Good stories reveal as much, or more, about a locale as any map or guidebook. Whereabouts Press is dedicated to publishing books that will enlighten a traveler to the soul of a place. By bringing a country's stories to the English-speaking reader, we hope to convey its culture through literature. Books from Whereabouts Press are essential companions for the curious traveler, and for the person who appreciates how fine writing enhances one's experiences in the world.

"Coming newly into Spanish, I lacked two essentials—a childhood in the language, which I could never acquire, and a sense of its literature, which I could."

—Alastair Reid, *Whereabouts: Notes on Being a Foreigner*

PRAGUE

A TRAVELER'S LITERARY COMPANION

EDITED BY
PAUL WILSON

WHEREABOUTS PRESS
BERKELEY, CALIFORNIA

Copyright © 1995 by Whereabouts Press
(complete copyright information on page 240)

ALL RIGHTS RESERVED

Published in the United States by
Whereabouts Press
Berkeley, California
www.whereaboutspress.com

Distributed to the trade by
Consortium Book Sales & Distribution
St. Paul, Minnesota

Manufactured in the United States of America

Library of Congress Cataloging-in-Publication Data

Prague : a traveler's literary companion /
edited by Paul Wilson.
p.   cm. — (Traveler's literary companions)
Includes bibliographical references.
ISBN 1-883513-01-4
1. Prague (Czech Republic) — Description and travel.
I. Wilson, Paul (Paul R.).   II. Series.
DB2614.P73   1995
914-371'20443—dc20   94-48122

10 9 8 7 6

To the memory of Emil Sobička,
who lived in all but the last of the many Pragues
in this century;

and for Jake,
who knows only the latest of its incarnations.

Contents

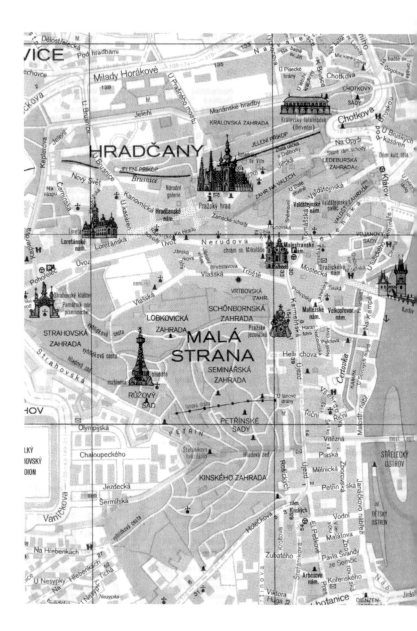

Preface

FOR THE LAST THOUSAND YEARS, Prague — or Praha, as the Czechs call her — has drawn people in mysterious and powerful ways, and held them enchanted. Even in its bright, new post-Communist wardrobe, Prague is a city where visitors can still experience something of the ancient magnetism that charmed both commoners and kings over the centuries, and feel aftershocks of the upheavals that have made it a place like no other on earth. As Franz Kafka once remarked, and as thousands of travelers are now discovering, Prague is still "a little mother that has claws." It is a city of stability in turmoil.

The turbulence of Prague is the turbulence of a troubled history flowing through a valley of high ideals and lofty aspirations. Enlightened emperors who might have ruled their domains from grander seats of power have chosen to place their thrones in Prague, and encouraged scholars, artists, and architects to come and raise the edifices of stone, images, and ideas on which the "city of a hundred spires" is built. Tyrants too, have held sway here, and perhaps because they felt threatened by the very lightness of the city in its good times, they created ponderous empires of darkness that sought to crush and enslave her spirit and her people. As a result, the city's history has a unique rhythm, an ebb and flow of radiant optimism and dark despair, that brings to the spirit of Prague a black humor tempered with gentle irony, sentiment without sentimentality, a sense of romance without romanticism, a skepticism without cynicism.

Prague is far more than the sum of its physical parts or its history. It is a city of the mind and the imagination, a city that exists as vividly in poetry and painting and music and legend as it does in brick and stone. But of all the arts that have shaped her, none has the antiquity, the roots, and the vigor of storytelling. Just as the physical city of Prague would be unimaginable without its unique topography, without its palaces, its churches, its parks, its streets, and its hostelries, so the Prague of the mind would be unimaginable without its storytellers and the tales they weave. It would be inconceivable without the work of Jan Neruda, who breathed literary life into a whole quarter of Prague, Malá Strana; or Franz Kafka, who sold insurance by day and beetled away at his true vocation by night, writing his strange, absurdist tales in German; or his contemporary Jaroslav Hašek, author of *The Good Soldier Švejk*, who led the life of a bon vivant and wrote his satirical sketches in the same city as Kafka, but in a parallel and largely separate community that lived and wrote in Czech; or Karel Čapek, the prophetic journalist, playwright, and novelist who introduced the world to robots; or Bohumil Hrabal, whose stories capture the extraordinary lives and voices of ordinary Czechs ruminating aloud over their beer. These storytellers embody Prague the way Dickens embodies London, Victor Hugo embodies Paris, or O. Henry embodies New York.

The stories in this anthology were written, roughly speaking, over the course of the past century. Some of them are classic tales by well-known authors, but more than half are by relatively unknown writers and, as far as I can determine, appear here in English for the first time. To qualify, a story had first of all to tell an entertaining tale in which the city of Prague itself figured as a backdrop or a setting. The stories had to be about people — some real, some imaginary, some famous, some ordinary — whose lives are enmeshed in different ways in the life of the city. Some are autobiographical, some are clearly fiction, and some are blends of fact and fantasy. Others are pure legend, yet they reveal a deeper truth about the soul of the city than straight history could.

An old friend once told me that though he had lived his entire life in Prague, he had, in fact, been a citizen of seven different countries. The oldest writer in the collection, Jan Neruda, died over a century ago, when Prague was a provincial city in the Austro-Hungarian Empire; the youngest, Jáchym Topol, was barely three years old when the Soviet Army invaded the Czechoslovak Socialist Republic in 1968. Over the period spanned by the stories in this book, Prague has been the jewel in the crown of a kingdom and an empire, a backwater town, the booming, industrial heart of a modern monarchy, the capital city of a new multi-national democracy, the dark, occupied center of a territory ruled, almost successively, by two oppressive totalitarian systems, the capital city of a new federal democracy, and finally, since January 1, 1993, the center of the Czech Republic of Bohemia, Moravia, and Silesia. Had my friend lived to see the fall of Communism, he could have added two more countries to his list.

I have also tried to give the reader a sample of the different cultures that have coexisted in Prague over the centuries, for though Prague is now the center of an almost exclusively Czech nation, it is far from being a purely Czech city. Since the Middle Ages, the Jewish and the German influences have been as powerful as the Slavic. A collection of this sort, however, can only hint at the important contributions the constituant cultures made to the general culture of the city. Writers like Gustav Meyrink, who is German, Egon Erwin Kisch and Franz Kafka, who are German and Jewish, and Jiří Weil and Ota Pavel, who are Jewish and write in Czech, may give the reader some idea of the range of Prague writing.

Gathering material for this book has been rather like trying to pick the perfect bouquet from a large field filled with beautiful flowers. There is only so much you can gather at once, and what you end up bringing home depends on the season, the climate, and even the time of day. Had I attempted such a collection before the collapse of Communism in 1989, it might have been a gloomier and perhaps duller looking bouquet, and I might have tried harder to represent the courageous authors who attempted to make sense of the totalitarian experience at considerable risk to their freedom. As it is, it felt like a real luxury to be able to make my selections without a sense of duty to anyone but the reader.

I should point out that the best known Czech literary hero, the good soldier Švejk, is absent from this book, although his author is not. For years, Jaroslav Hašek's classic comic novel about the bumbling loyalist whose absurdly exaggerated sense of duty brings chaos to the Austrian army was the only work of Czech literature guaranteed to be available in English in every bookstore. Nor is there anything in the collection by one of the best-known Czech writers, Milan Kundera, because Kundera is not really a Prague author, having spent most of his life either in Brno, or in Paris. And one of the classic novels of the pre-1968 Communist era, *Summer in Prague*, by Zdena Salivarová, is so delightfully dense that proved beyond my capacities to excerpt. My conscience is eased because most of what I have left out is still in print, and available in English to those whose appetites are whetted, but not satisfied, by the present collection.

In the months of hunting and gathering that have resulted in this volume, I have had many reliable and helpful guides. My thanks to Petr Pithart, Jaroslav Med, Viktor Stoilov, Jan Šulc, Dr. Miloslav Žilina, Jan Zelenka, Andrej and Olga Stankovič, Rob Wechsler, Josef Škvorecky, Zdena Salivarová, Zdeněk Urbánek, Eda Kriseová, Andrzej Jagodzinski and Katarzyna Borun-Jagodzinska, Richard Partington, George Brady, Anna Mozga, Marketa Goetz-Stankeiwicz, Elena Lappin, and Alison Gzowski. These people provided inspiration, advice, material support, and encouragement, sometimes all at once. I would like to give special thanks to my assistant Patricia Grant, who worked with me closely every step of the way.

I am grateful as well to the translators with whom I worked directly: Norma Comrada, Michael Henry Heim, Peter Kussi, Gerry and Alice Turner, Marie Winn, and Alex Zucker, both for their excellent work, but equally for their ideas and suggestions about what material to include. In that sense, the book is theirs as well, although I accept full responsibility for its shortcomings. Translating from Czech used to be a lonely profession, by and large, and one of the best things about the return of freedom has been the arrival of talented new translators on the scene. This can only bode well for the future of Czech writing in the world.

Paul Wilson
Toronto, November 1994

I See a Great City . . .

Daniela Hodrová

IN THE BEGINNING, the city was a word — *Praha*. Somewhat later, lying in my crib, I watched the bands of light that flickered across the ceiling whenever a streetcar went by. I imagined the city as a predatory beast, asleep somewhere far away. (In childhood, I felt that our apartment building was on the periphery of the city, although in reality it was only a half-hour's walk from the center.) The breath of this beast, hot and exotic, would sometimes waft through the window, washing over me like a wave. But the beast was not asleep in its lair, it was lying in wait.

It was only later, when I had left my crib with its metal bars and went for the first time onto our fifth-floor balcony — where a few years before a Jewish girl had jumped to her death to avoid being taken away on the transports — that the word, which had so far been the name of the beast, became the uncertain, alluring, and disturbing space that lay before me when I looked out. At first I thought the city was no more than this broad expanse, this dark vale surrounded on four sides by walls. For the tenement house of my childhood stood right across the street from the largest Prague cemetery — the Olšanský Cemetery — and the window of my room looked out over it. On All Hallows' Eve and other holy days, the cemetery became a transoceanic liner, shimmering with countless points of light, sailing past my window like the boat in Fellini's *Amarcord*.

If I try to evoke my primordial perception of the city, I do so, perhaps, under the impression that Prague arose from nothingness, parallel with my arrival in the world and my acquisition of consciousness. The space in which it grew took on its present contours only before my birth. When the hands of my grandfather, the head physician Dr. Jan Jerie, guided me into the world in the Bubeneč Sanatorium, an ancient sea still filled the Prague basin, its bottom riddled by volcanic eruptions. The hardening lava formed the stony out-cropping above the Prokop Valley, the Vyšehrad Rock, and the Karlov promontory. Trilobites and other prehistoric crea-tures discovered in the last century by the French geologist Joachim Barrande were petrified within these rocks. The seas in those ancient times, which corresponded to the first days of my life, still covered the place where the Olšanský Ceme-tery would rise in a time of plague, and they washed against the building in which we lived, in a flat that once belonged to a German family who left behind, in my room, a puppet theater with a blue velvet curtain.

Then the sea began to recede. The cellar walls sparkled with crystals of salt that the superintendent's son, Peter N., and I tested with our tongues. At that time, the building was to me what the whole city gradually became — hell, purga-tory, and paradise, or rather merely an underworld, for the borders between those individual areas were imperceptible. Is this not one of the qualities that characterizes this city as a whole — that blending of places of mercy with places of dam-nation?

And the sea receded further. Lo, from the darkness of ancient times the Vltava River emerged, its tributaries carv-ing the valleys that come down to meet it. And then the river slowly sank from the height of the ridges that border the Prague basin, leaving a layer of alluvia at Flora, Olšany, the Pankrác plateau, and the Bohnice heights. The waters gradually declined to the level of Charles Square and Vodičkova Street. And when I first stood on my feet in the wooden playpen in the middle of my room, hunters appeared in the Prague basin to stalk wild animals in the virgin forest, take honey from the trunks of linden trees, and offer sacrifices to demons where their trails crossed. Then came the ceramic-pottery people and after them, the bow-and-arrow people, who drank from bell-shaped goblets. At the end of the fourth century before Christ, the Celts appeared and after them, almost at the beginning of our era, the Markomans. It is only then that the Slavs arrived. That would be about the time our maid Anežka, who had a hump, would take me every afternoon in a cream-white baby carriage past the walls of the Olšanský Cemetery. They worshipped idols, prayed to their ancestors. Sacred trees rustled above the flames that blazed over the bonfires of the dead. They danced around their fires in masks. The stench of the victims' smoking blood reached the child in her baby carriage.

LIBUŠE'S PROPHECY

The city was a word, a beast lying in wait, a sea that slowly receded. It was a house where Peter N. waited for me in the cellar. And it was also my father, who would lean over me in the middle of the night after coming back from the Vinohrady Theater. His face smelled of makeup and Vaseline. (The smell of the theater alternated with the smell of exotic fruit the city gave off when I was still an infant.) From those times on, the city has been associated in some mysterious way in my mind with theater; the city and the theater are one and the same, and together they form a kind of sacred scene — a *vision* — that appears when the curtain is raised. The curtain of this theater-city is to be found, I think, somewhere around the National Museum, where the Horse Gate once stood, at the top of the square dominated by the statue of St. Wenceslas. Before an audience standing on the museum staircase, above the fountain that no longer flows, the curtain is raised and living scenes begin to unfold. In any case, the sloping square itself resembles a stage. It does not, however, slope towards the audience on the museum steps, as it usually does in theaters, but in the opposite direction, toward Můstek. Where the prompter's box is located in classical theaters, there stood for many years, on May Day, a reviewing stand draped in red cloth. From this spot presidents would deliver speeches and the people parading below it would greet them with cheers and applause, which dwindled over the years until finally this living scene was moved to another reviewing stand — on the Plains of Letna, where a circus is now located.

Wenceslas Square — the stage of a living theater. Some of the scenes I merely imagine, others actually took place.

SCENE ONE: *Slavs on the territory of Bohemia.* An idyllic scene from the life of the ancient Slavs. They live in fortified settlements on the territory of the future city. The princes wear robes embroidered in purple and gold and sit on their thrones in colonnaded halls. In Vyšehrad or in Opyš — where the Castle will one day stand.

SCENE TWO: *Libuše's prophecy.* Princess Libuše puts the purple robe on Přemysl, whom, according to the legend, she had summoned to the throne from his plow. The princess stands on the staircase of the museum in a ceremonial gown with a diadem on her head, like a Byzantine monarch. She holds a linden branch in her hands and, eyes aflame, gazes somewhere over the tunnel to the Main Station. She prophecies: *I see a great city, whose glory will reach to the stars.* That is how the medieval chronicler, Kosmas, put it down in Latin. In Smetana's opera *Libuše,* performed on gala occasions in the National Theater, Libuše strangely does not predict glory for the future city. After several Czech rulers, the Hussites, and finally Jiří of Poděbrady appear before her, she sings: *And what then? Mist shrouds my eyes and much is hidden from my troubled sight — terrible secrets, curses. . . .* In the president's box sits Tomáš Garrigue Masaryk, and after him Edvard Beneš, then Klement Gottwald, then Emil Zápotocký, then Antonín Novotný, then Ludvík Svoboda, then Gustav Husák, then Václav Havel. And the princess sings on: *My beloved Czech people shall not perish, but shall triumph o'er the horrors of hell.* The chorus then joins in: *The Czech people shall not perish, but shall triumph o'er the horrors of hell! Glory!* Only President Hácha, a puppet manipulated by the Germans under the Protectorate, did not hear Libuše's prophecy from this box, because the opera was banned during the war. He may, however, have heard it from the yard of the Pankrác Prison, when they took their mad prisoner out into the sun when the war was over. *The Czech people shall not perish . . . the horrors of hell. . . .* The composer himself never heard a note of his aria; by 1873, when he finished the opera, he was stone deaf. In the early years of the dark fifties, shortly after Gottwald's death, men from the secret service raided the villa of Professor Haškovec and dumped a bottle containing Smetana's brain

down the toilet. Mistakenly? Deliberately? I see a great city
... which shall triumph o'er the horrors of hell! Glory! ...

THE ST. WENCESLAS GAME

From ancient times, the dominating feature of this city was
the Gothic cathedral that stands against the sky over the river.
In 1989, where the old Jewish cemetery used to be in the
Mahler gardens in Žižkov, an enormous television tower
emerged from the rubble of rooftops. The deadly white stem
of this gigantic stinkhorn mushroom *(Phallus impudicus),* as
my husband dubbed it, became a new, false landmark. Its
shadow falls across the Cathedral of the Sacred Heart and
across the roof of the building in which I have lived since I
was thirteen. Sometimes I feel it has, like a mushroom,
sprung up overnight, and will one day rot away. That, however, has not yet happened. One autumn day that year, the
arm of an enormous crane suddenly appeared outside my
window. The orange-green tentacle with two men in it
moved slowly along the street and the men looked into my
window as I was writing. Their faces were expressionless. Below, in the street, a small crowd of people had gathered to
watch their incomprehensible activity. To this day, I don't
know if it was a coincidence, or whether it was related to the
case that was being heard in the courthouse in Jagellonská
Street. They had just put Václav Havel on trial.

One other thing made me uneasy that autumn. A rumor was going round that somewhere outside Prague, in
Hrdlořezy, the Black Berets, a special emergency police unit,
had built a second Wenceslas Square complete with Mezi-
branská, Ve Smečkách, Vodičkova, and other side streets, and

the National Museum. They even put up a replica of St. Wenceslas, but they say it was crudely hacked out of wood, and the saint was without his horse, and without his suite of patrons. Day after day, they played the St. Wenceslas game, as I call it, in Hrdlořezy. It is played this way: a wall of men with shields guards the statue. Anyone who breaks through the barrier, wishing to become St. Wenceslas, is beaten. Reality had strangely begun to replicate itself, or was it just that I had not noticed this before?

Other things happened that year too. One day, in the courtyard of the Strahov Cloister, which houses the National Literary Archives with its famous library and the Literary Institute where I work, the Czech lion appeared, the model for a statue that had been hidden from the public for years. Unlike the lion that lies peacefully in the bend of the Chotkova Road winding up to the Castle, the Strahov lion stands rampant, ready for battle — it is a roaring lion. For many long months this lion, which had emerged from the non-memory and the non-being of the nation, stood in the corner of the courtyard and foreign tourists would lie under the beast and take pictures of its enormous leonine penis, until finally one day, it was unceremoniously lifted up with a crane and set down on a base of crude stone blocks. In the manifestation of this beast of prey, though it became an object of carnival laughter, it was possible to sense a promise.

THE MAGIC OF WORDS

Something was at work in the reality of the city, something the policemen who played the Wenceslas Game in Hrdlořezy and later on the anniversaries of August 21 and October 28 on the real Wenceslas Square hadn't counted on: the magic of words. In his *Experimental Psychology*, Břetislav Kafka writes about a peculiar envelope surrounding the Earth made up of the feelings, thoughts, and memories of all the living, and of those long since dead. Are not cities surrounded by a similar envelope? And does it too consist not just of all the lives of its citizens, but of all the myths and prophecies ever connected with the city, all those ever written or — if we admit the existence of black holes and loops in time — those as yet unwritten as well? . . .

November came, and with it, the Velvet Revolution. Almost overnight, the city roused itself from its fatal lassitude, from its half-being and half-consciousness. Real people bled in the place where my fictional characters had shed blood. The city came alive with words. Words covered the shop windows, the walls, the halls, and the corridors of the subway, which until that point had been a silent mausoleum to the ruling ideology. Then, upon entering the subway one day when the students had just taken down all the signs and erased all the words, I was overcome with a moment of doubt. What if this had all been just a dream — the kind in which the prisoner dreams that he has become king? A dream it happily was not, or if it was, I have not yet awakened from it.

AUTUMN 1990

Translated from the Czech by Paul Wilson

Bells

Jiří Karásek ze Lvovic

HE WANDERED ONTO PETŘÍN HILL and looked down at the city. He derived no more from the view than the impression of a vague, tumultuous space. A great weariness ascended from it all. Everything seemed vain and empty. What was colorful merged with the colorless, the clear with the dark, the light with the shadows. He stood there a long time, without a thought, his eyes transfixed. . . .

He was suddenly disturbed by the approach of someone who appeared as reclusive and solitary as he. The stranger sat down on the bench close to him and involuntarily, the two men looked at each other. Something seemed to draw them together at once, yet they did not speak and indeed, they scarcely dared give each other a second glance.

But from that moment on he felt under the magnetic influence of the new arrival. Might this person be a friend?

Ah, to live, only to live. . . . Anything but this stale existence, this half-life. Nothing was whole and entire, nothing substantial. No real passions, no real emotions, not even real boredom. Nothing but half-feelings, half-passions, half-boredom. Someone would smile at him as he passed by, yet he knew not why they smiled. Someone would say: Come with me, and he would follow, with no idea why, or where. That was the sum of it. And that was life. What was it all for? Pure folly, pure self-torment for the sake of an unattainable chimera.

From *Gothic Spirit*, first published in 1900.

A setting ray of sunshine swirled the golden dust in the air, and then went out; twilight veiled the forms of the city. Orange shadows settled on the tiled rooftops, in the old courtyards, in the gardens abloom with hawthorn.

He looked abruptly into the stranger's eyes. In the gathering dusk their greenish tint faded to a soft, languid amber, exuding warmth that seemed to drink in the darkness. These were eyes that attracted and yet mocked, half-open, half-closed, now with a sharpened alertness, again with utter indifference. He felt an uneasy affection for the stranger and longed to possess his secret. He observed the movements of his lips and the nervous trembling of his fingers, and at once he seemed strangely familiar. His lips were no longer the lips of a stranger, but his own lips, and the hands — they were his hands. He identified with him and seemed hypnotized by him, so that everything around them seemed weary and sleepy. . . .

And now the evening bells began to ring out over Prague. A dead weight, dark, metallic, and tragic, fell from their polyphony. The air was replete with an unexpected pall. Slumbering shadows smothered the rooftops. Not a feather, not a bird, moved in the evening air. It was as though everything were suddenly alarmed and alert to the conversation of the bells. And the clangor broke free from the windows of belfry and spire, the reverberations poured into the air, grew fainter with the distance, and faltered over the rooftops. As in a memory, everything now seemed to acquire a voice of its own, the tiles on the rooftops, the crooked chimneys, the rotting window frames, the blind panes of glass, the darkened gables, the crumbling cornices. Prague, its past, began speaking in bells under the descending twilight. . . .

He felt the distant dead speaking through the bells, as if innumerable legions of invisible ghosts had come alive and were thronging the city streets and moving about inside the houses.

Everything spoke to him of multitudes who had lived here before him, who had had the same longings as he, and finally passed into nothingness. Their hands had also trembled with the fever of discontent. Their pulses had quickened at the approach of mystery. They had wanted to love, and instead they inflicted pain. They had wanted to be loved, and instead felt coldness. Their souls had opened to the amplitude and the profundity of life, and in the end they had known only their own pettiness.

He was an inheritor of the dead. All who lived here were inheritors of the past. They had the eyes, the voices, the hands of the distant dead. They had their desires, their passions. The whole history of the country was but a constant renewal of the selfsame generation, engaged on some secret business, throwing themselves on each other's mercy while no one enjoyed a vision of the whole.

And the bells rang on.

They spoke of the faded glory of this land, the feuds of its princes and the onslaughts of its enemies against the walls of the city. They spoke of the arrogant burghers and the dissolute priests, its weak kings and perfideous vassals.

The tide of blood made the heavens blush. The great phantasmagoria of churches ablaze and monasteries in ruins rose up before his eyes. An enormous chalice stood out against the red sky. Vyšehrad collapsed. The walls of Hradčany crumbled. Malá Strana vanished in flames. The Carthusian monastery on Újezd was wrapped in the smoke of a conflagration. And the whole earth trembled as in an earthquake.

Then Prague grew calm once more. Cathedral walls rose up. Hradčany filled with the noisy life of the court. Then new catastrophes rolled in like thunderheads laden with horrors. Strahov Gate saw armies flee from the battlefield and the Old Town Square drank the blood of insurgents. An alien spirit entered the land and suffocated its life.

The bells of St. Vitus could be heard most clearly. The enormous Zigmund bell tolled a tragic knell, crushingly heavy, as if to make its voice heard in the deepest vaults of the cathedral where the dead kings slept. It was answered by the bells of Strahov and Loretta, an even melody of sound, a mood of distant, muffled tintinnabulation submerged in the gloom and the twilight. Below him the bells of St. Nicholas pealed forth with a voice that seemed flattened in some dark depth. The Maltese bells sounded darkest of all, as though trapped for eternity in the rubble of the spire.

From across the river rang the knell of the Týn bells, invoking new horrors on the place of execution. The Jindřišská bells groaned as they once had under the barrage of Swedish and Prussian cannonballs. The bells of the Franciscan monastery recalled the devastated cathedral and the murdered monks, and their voices were heavy with numb oppression. In Karlova Street the cupola swayed with the sound of its carillon as though recalling the storms that had once shaken it. The bells of Vyšehrad were faint in the boundless distance, as though from a long-since vanished cathedral. The Štěpanské bells wept over the tombstones of families now extinct.

And scarcely audible, the bells of abolished churches, long silenced, seemed to blend into the chorale. Now, in the twilight, buildings transformed ages ago into tenements, hospitals, offices, private dwellings, and warehouses were suddenly cloaked in their former aspect as ancient temples and cloisters. The people walking in the winding, melancholy, shadowy streets suddenly assumed unexpected forms. Their pace slowed and they were garbed in long, flowing cloaks that made them seem taller. Their faces, stark and cadaverous, emerged from starched ruffled collars shaded by broad-brimmed hats.

The Middle Ages came alive in streets that narrowed in the darkness, pressing the rows of silent houses together. Night gave the city back its former shape and, for an instant, transformed the memory of its ancient glory into reality.

He looked down on the city, transfixed.

His eyes took in all that so many before him had seen, so many lives from long lost times. He felt their disembodied being on the damp, mildewed walls. He sensed their touch adhering to the stones, the doors and windows. He merged his being with the spirits of those dead, with the rhythm of their breath. He called them forth and brought them back to life, though nothing remained of them now but the anonymous dust a gale will lift and scatter throughout the city, coating the paving stones, the roofs, gathering in the corners.

He awoke from his trance and with great effort returned to the present. He felt the strangeness and the vagueness of everything. There was something hard and unyielding in his relation to things and his separateness from the rest of the world.

Everything long since past, but which waited in the background like an inexorable phantom, he now sensed as the agonizing bedrock of his present life. It would be impossible, he felt, to shake off this feeling here, in this city.

He rose to his feet and found himself completely alone. The stranger had gone. A dead silence spread across the city. The heavens had turned a dark cobalt blue. He now felt something like an abrupt regret for the stranger. . . .

Translated from the Czech by Paul Wilson

The First Vision

Gustav Meyrink

MY PEN CAN HARDLY KEEP PACE with all the experiences and apparitions that threaten to overwhelm me. I use the quiet hours of the night to record all that has happened to me.

Then I took up John Dee's *Lapis sacer et praecipuus manifestationis* and contemplated the stand and the inscription on it. Gradually my eye began to wander from the gold ornamentation to the oily surface of the coal itself. What then began to happen was similar — at least, so it seems to me in retrospect — to my experience when I looked into Lipotin's Florentine mirror, and dreamed I was standing at the station waiting for my friend Gartner.

However that may be, after some time staring at the shining black surface of the crystal, I found I could no longer take my eyes off it. I saw — or rather, I did not so much see as feel I was in the middle of a herd of milk-white horses galloping wildly over a surface of green-black waves. At first I thought — and I might add that my thoughts were clear and rational — aha, Johanna's green sea! But after a short while I began to see the details more precisely and I realized that the riderless horses were rushing over night-dark woods and meadows like Woden's wild hunt. At the same time I knew that these were the souls of the millions upon millions of men who are asleep in their beds while their souls, without rider, without

From *The Angel of the West Window.*

master, are driven by some dark instinct to seek their far-off, unknown home — they do not know where it lies, they only sense they have lost it and cannot find it again.

I myself was a rider on a snow-white steed that seemed more real, more corporeal, than the milk-white horses. The frenzied, snorting mustangs — they were like crests of foam on a stormy sea — crossed some wooded hills that disappeared below us in long waves. In the distance was the narrow silver ribbon of a meandering river.

A wide landscape opens out like an amphitheater embroidered with ranges of low hills. The furious gallopade is heading for the river. In the distance the mass of a city begins to rise. The bounding shapes of the horses around me seem to dissolve into gray clouds of mist. Then, all of a sudden, I am riding through the bright sunshine of an August morning, across a stone bridge with tall statues of saints and kings on the parapet. On the river bank I am approaching modest dwellings huddled together in an ancient jumble with a few magnificent palaces towering above them, and, so to speak, shouldering them to one side; but even these proud edifices are humbled by the immense bulk of a tree-covered hill crowned with ramparts pierced by the outlines of towers, roofs, battlements, and spires. A voice within me cries: "Hradčany! The Castle!"

I am in Prague, then? Who is in Prague? Who am I? What is going on all around me? I can see myself on horseback, scarcely attracting a second glance from the townsfolk and peasants who are likewise crossing the stone bridge over the Vltava, past the statue of St. Nepomuk and on to the Malá Strana, the lesser town. I know I have been commanded to appear before the Emperor Rudolf — Rudolf of Hapsburg — in the Belvedere. Beside me, on a dapple-gray mare, rides my companion; in spite of the blue sky and scorching sun he is encased in a fur cloak of somewhat tarnished magnificence. The fur coat is obviously the pièce de résistance of his wardrobe and he has donned it in order to make some kind of show before His Majesty. "A mountebank's finery," I think. It does not surprise me to find that I myself am wearing antiquated dress. How could it be otherwise! Is it not the feast of St. Lawrence, the tenth day of August in the year of Our Lord, 1583? I have ridden back into the past, I tell myself, and find nothing odd about it.

The man with the mouse's eyes, the low forehead, and receding chin is Edward Kelley, whom I had difficulty in restraining from taking rooms at the inn at the sign of the Last Lantern, where the immensely rich magnates and archdukes stay when they come to court. He keeps our common purse, and he is as full of himself as a fairground quack. Completely shameless and correspondingly successful, he constantly manages to fill our coffers at times when a gentleman would rather cut off his hand or lie down in a ditch to die. I know — I am John Dee, my own ancestor bearing a letter of introduction to the Emperor Rudolf from Queen Elizabeth. And now I am living in Prague with my wife, child, and Kelley in the spacious house of His Majesty's learned personal physician, Doctor Tomaš Hájek, in the center of the Old Town.

Today, then, is the day, so important for me, of my first audience with the prince among adepts and the adept among kings — the mysterious, feared, hated, and revered Rudolf. Beside me, Edward Kelley exudes self-confidence and sets his horse at a tripping canter, but my heart is heavy with foreboding. I feel the dark nature of the emperor hanging over me like the black cloud that is just passing across the gleaming façade of the castle above us. At the end of the bridge our horses' hooves echo as we ride through the gaping maw of a gloomy gatehouse. Behind us, closed off as if by a wall, lies the bright world of ordinary, cheerful folk. Steep, joyless alleys climb up silently between houses cowering fearfully against the hillside. Black palaces bar the way, like gatekeepers of the ominous secrets that surround Hradčany Castle. But now the broad esplanade, which the emperor's bold architect has blasted out of the hill and wrested from the narrow wooded gorge, opens up before us. Away on a distant hilltop the defiant towers of a monastery rise up. "Strahov!" a voice within me says — Strahov that conceals, buried alive within its mute walls, many a man who was struck by a fateful bolt from the emperor's eyes, and who yet can consider himself fortunate that he did not have to make the nocturnal journey down that other narrow alley to Dalibor's tower, when he could say farewell forever to the light of the stars. The houses of the imperial servants are piled up on top of each other, like swallows' nests on a cliff, each one bracing itself on the one below. At all costs the Hapsburgers want to have their German bodyguard close around them; they will not trust themselves to the teeming alien race down there across the Vltava. Hradčany Castle towers above the city with bristling defenses; every gateway echoes with the jingle of spurs, the clash of ever-ready weapons. We ride slowly up the hill. Suspicious eyes follow us from the tiny windows above. Three times already we have been unexpectedly stopped by guards who suddenly appear from nowhere to ask us our business. The emperor's letter granting us audience is checked again and again. Then we are out on the splendid approach, the city of Prague spread out below us. I look at the view like a prisoner gazing out on the free world. Up here everything seems to be in the tight grip of an invisible hand. Up here the summit of the hill has become a prison! The city below seems to lie in a sea of silver dust. Above us the sun smolders through a misty veil. All of a sudden silver streaks appear in the powdery blue of the sky. Flocks of doves circle round in the still air, reflecting the light, and then disappear behind the spires of the Týn Church. Not a sound . . . it is unreal. But I take the doves over Prague as a good omen. The bell of the high-vaulted cathedral of St. Nicholas below strikes ten; from somewhere within the ramparts of the stronghold in front of us a sharp, imperative clock repeats the hour with a swift drumroll — it is high time! The monarch, a fanatical collector of clocks, keeps to the precise second. Woe to anyone who appears late! Another fifteen minutes, I think, and I shall be standing before Rudolf.

We have reached the top and could set our steeds at a gallop were it not for the halberdiers that block our every step; there is no end to the checks and scrutiny. Finally the bridge over the deer moat thunders beneath our horses' hooves, and we are trotting across the quiet park of the hermit king.

Surrounded by ancient oaks, the green copper roof of the airy Belvedere rises before us like a huge upturned ship's hull. We jump down from our horses.

The first things to attract my eye are the stone reliefs on the balustrade of the loggia formed by delicate arches around the Belvedere. There is Samson wrestling with the lion and, opposite, Hercules overcoming the Nemean lion. They are the symbols that the emperor chooses to guard the entrance to his ultimate refuge. It is well known that the lion is his favorite animal and that he has trained a huge African lion as a pet with which he likes to frighten even his intimates. All around it is deserted and silent. No one to receive us?! A bell with a note like a crystal goblet sounds the quarter. Clocks even here!

At the last stroke a plain wooden door opens. Wordlessly, a gray-haired servant invites us to enter. Stable boys suddenly appear to take our horses. We are standing in the long, cool hall of the Belvedere Palace. The stench of camphor is suffocating. The whole room is piled high with glass cases full of strange, exotic specimens: life-size models of savages in bizarre poses going about their bizarre business, weapons, gigantic animals, all kinds of implements, Chinese flags, Indian totem poles, an abundance of curiosities from the Old and the New World. At a sign from our guide we stop beside the immense nightmare figure of a shaggy wood wight with a satanically grinning skull. Kelley's bravura has withdrawn to the inmost recesses of his fur. He whispers some nonsense about evil spirits. I have to smile at the mountebank who does not tremble at all before his own conscience, but cowers in fear of a stuffed gorilla.

But at that very same moment I feel my bowels gripped with a shock of fear as a black ghost floats soundlessly around the corner beyond the ape's case and a scrawny figure faces us. Yellow hands pull a shabby black gown tight around him and fidget under the folds with a weapon. The outline of a short dagger is clear to see. A pale birdlike head is lit by yellow eagle's eyes. The emperor!

The thin, creased upper lip is drawn tight over the almost toothless gums, but the heavy lower lip hangs slack and bluish over the firm chin. The beady predator's eyes survey us. He remains silent.

I kneel — just a second too late, it seems. Then as we kneel before him, heads bowed, he waves his hand dismissively.

"Stuff and nonsense. Stand up, if you call yourself honest men. Otherwise go to the devil and do not waste any more of my time."

Such was the greeting of the sublime emperor.

I begin the speech that I had carefully composed long before. I have hardly mentioned the gracious intercession of my mighty queen when the emperor interrupts me impatiently.

"Let me see what you can do! My envoys bring me more than enough greetings from other rulers. You claim to possess the tincture?"

"More than that, Your Majesty."

"What, more?" Rudolf hisses. "Insolence will get you nowhere with me!"

"It is humility, not presumption, that leads us to take refuge in the wisdom of a high adept. . . ."

"I know a little. Enough to warn you not to try to deceive me."

"I seek only the truth, Your Majesty, not self-enrichment."

"The truth?!" A malicious smile flickers across the old man's face. "I am not such a fool as Pilate to ask you, 'What is truth?' What I want to know is, have you the tincture?"

"Yes, Your Majesty."

"Out with it!"

Kelley pushes to the front. He carries the white sphere from St. Deiniol's grave in a leather bag hidden in the depths of his jerkin.

"If Your Most Gracious Majesty will only put us to the test!" His obsequiousness is crude.

"Who is that? Your assistant, your medium, I presume?"

"My colleague and friend, Edward Kelley," I answer, sensing a spurt of irritation within.

"A quack by trade, I see," hisses the emperor. The ancient

eagle eye, weary from having seen too much, scarcely acknowledges the apothecary. The latter grovels like a scolded urchin and is silent.

I try once more: "If Your Majesty would deign to hear me."

To our surprise Rudolf signals to an old servant, who brings a hard folding stool. The emperor sits down and, with a curt nod, gives me permission to continue.

"Your Majesty wants to know about the tincture for making gold. We have the tincture, but we have — and we are striving for — more. I hope to God we are worthy of it."

"What could be more precious than the philosopher's stone?" the emperor snaps.

"Wisdom, Your Majesty!"

"Are you canting priests?"

"We seek to be worthy to be counted with Your Majesty among the adepts."

"And what are you counting on?" The emperor's tone is mocking.

"On the angel who commands us."

"And what kind of angel is that?"

"It is the angel . . . of the West Gate."

The emperor's eye, that seems to see a world beyond ours, is hooded. "What does this angel command you to do?"

"The twofold alchemy, the transmutation of mortal to immortal, the way of Elijah."

"Do you mean to ride up to heaven in a fiery chariot like the old Jew? There was one who tried it before. He broke his neck."

"The angel teaches us no fairground tricks, Your Majesty. He teaches us how to preserve the body beyond the grave. I can supply the Imperial Lodge of Adepts with evidence and proof."

"Is that all you can do?" The emperor seems to be falling asleep. Kelley is becoming impatient.

"We can do more. The stone that we possess can transmute any metal . . ."

The emperor's head shoots up: "Proof!"

Kelley pulls out his leather bag. "Your Lordship may command. I am ready."

"You seem a reckless knave, but of a quicker wit than your companion!"

I choke back the rising indignation. The Emperor Rudolf is no adept! He wants to see gold made! The vision of the angel and its gifts — the secret of incorruptibility — mean nothing to him, indeed, are a mockery to him. Does he follow the way of the left hand? Then the emperor suddenly says, "First of all let a man change base metal into gold that I can hold in my hand, then let him talk to me of angels. A schemer is touched by neither God nor the devil."

I cannot say why, but his words cut me to the quick. With a swifter movement than would seem possible for such an aged, sickly figure, the emperor sits up. The neck shoots forward, on it the eagle's head jerks from side to side, searching for prey. Finally it nods at the wall.

A concealed door suddenly opens before our eyes.

A few seconds later we are standing in the emperor's tiny laboratory. It is well supplied with equipment of all kinds. The crucible sits over a well-stoked fire. Everything is soon made ready. With a practiced hand the emperor himself carries out the assistant's tasks, gruffly refusing our attempts to help. His suspicion is boundless. His meticulous precautions would be the despair of any trickster. It is impossible to deceive him. Suddenly there is a faint clash of weapons. Behind the hidden door — I can sense it — lurks death. Rudolf deals summarily with any wandering mountebanks who dare to try and hoodwink him.

Kelley turns pale and looks at me for help. I can sense what is going through his mind: What if the powder fails now? He is seized by the vagabond's fear.

Lead is bubbling in the crucible. Kelley unscrews the sphere, the emperor keeping a suspicious eye on him. Kelley touches the sphere, then hesitates.

The eagle's beak strikes, "I am no thief, pill-peddler! Give it to me."

Rudolf subjects the gray powder in the sphere to a long and searching examination. The mocking cast of his lips gradually relaxes, the bluish lower lip sags to his chin. The expression on the eagle's face becomes thoughtful. Kelley indicates the dosage. The emperor carries out every instruction precisely and conscientiously, like a well-trained laboratory assistant.

The lead is liquid. Now the emperor adds the tincture. The metal begins to froth. The emperor pours the "mother" into the cold bath. With his own hands he lifts the lump up to the light. There is a gleam of pure silver.

The leafy garden shimmers in the afternoon heat as Kelley and I ride through, exhilarated, almost cocky. Kelley jingles the silver chain that the emperor put around his neck this morning. The words of the emperor were, "Silver for silver, gold for gold, Doctor Quack. The next time will come the test whether you made the powder and whether you can make it again. The crown — note this well — is only for the adept. Chains indicate . . . chains."

Translated from the German by Mike Mitchell

What Shall We Do with It?

Jan Neruda

The Writer's Opening Prayer

"Heaven Almighty! Protect Thou my thoughts and guard my witticisms from arousing the displeasure of the high and mighty, offending the sensibilities and moral purity of my fellow citizens, and harming the sales of tomorrow's paper, for it is the Sunday edition. Amen!"

HAVE YOU EVER been in the street in the early morning, gentle reader? Not that I wish to insult you. I know that my readers *are* in fact gentle and have no need to rise before nine, but if, say, by chance. And if chance has lured you out of the house earlier than usual, surely you have been keen-sighted enough to observe that one finds things as well as people not otherwise seen there, and keen-witted enough to give some thought to those things and people, but primarily to the things: an old jug standing in front of a house, a milk can wound round with wire at the edge of the pavement, a baking pan in the middle of the road. How did they get there? Did they escape from unguarded shelves and then fail to find their way back home in the light of dawn? Or did they lose their cook during her morning rounds and decide to wait there like a well-trained dog which, having strayed from its master, will sit itself down even in the middle of the road and look this way and that until it is recovered?

Anyway, there is much talk nowadays about cholera — I beg the gentle reader to refrain from interrupting and inquiring after the connection with what has gone before, that is, to let me go on writing as I please, for in the end he shall see that I am less frivolous than he imagines. To repeat, there is much talk about cholera. About the ways one can go about preventing it. Mainly, the fact that keeping one's flat clean is half the battle. Though keeping the air disinfected is also half the battle. As is eating fresh, healthy beef, veal, and pork. And drinking good Pilsener beer. *Summa summarum* if one observes all the regulations, one is two and a half battles ahead of the game, that is, two and a half times healthier than necessary. And why not observe the regulations, when a) they have one's health at heart and b) following official regulations fills one with ineffable delight!

Thus, the moment I read the municipal decree posted on the nearest corner, I turned on my heel and went home. Well, well, I said to myself, the place is actually quite clean. The furniture and floor are under the careful constant care of my Anča; the books are under my own care, true, but a little dust never hurt a book — they even look ostentatious, overbearing, and silly when dusted. As for everything else, well, there isn't really anything else. Just the bed, and what could be cleaner than a bachelor's bed: pillows like two swans, a cover like a field of lilies, a sheet white as snow, a mattress puffy as a bun, a mattress stuffed with straw, with straw. . . .

"Anča!"

"Yes, sir?"

"When did I last change the straw in my mattress?"

"Can't say as I know. Not as long as I've been with you. Must be like sawdust by now."

Anča has been with me for six years. And when I try to think farther back, I draw a blank. I must have bought it, stuffed and stitched, while still in the blush of youth.

"Anča!"

"Yes, sir?"

"Here are seventy-five kreutzers. Go and buy me three trusses of straw. This very moment!"

Off she flies. She is back in no time dragging three trusses of straw. She grabs the mattress, undoes the stitching, and is about to start stuffing it when she freezes and says, "What do we do with the old straw?"

Women do have faster minds than men. It would have taken me forever to think of it! Of course. Before we put in the new straw, we have to remove the old, and — what shall we do with it? Toss it out of the window, on somebody's head?

"What *do* people do with old straw?"

"Can't say as I know."

"Hm," I say. "Here are six more kreutzers. Go over to the big house with the rubbish pit. Give the money to the care-taker, and he'll let you empty the straw into the pit." So men's minds are worth something after all!

Off she goes and back she comes. He won't let her, she says. The servant girls throw hot ashes into the pit and the straw might catch fire. Besides, the pit is almost full and the peasant who empties it is busy and can't come till winter.

"Then what shall we do?"

"Can't say as I know."

"Well. I know!" I cry out after a bit. The male mind is amazingly fertile. "Tomorrow is Wednesday, and Wednesday is rubbish day. Take the six kreutzers and give half to the rubbish man and half to the driver. They'll load it onto the cart."

"Fine, but what will your honor sleep on? I can't put the

mattress back on the bed. The stitching's open. The straw would fall through the boards."

"True. So I'll . . . then I'll . . . I'll just have to sleep on the floor. We'll take the long cushion off the sofa and lay it on the floor, make it up like a bed, and it will be superb. I'll sleep like a king."

And sleep like a king I did.

Next morning Anča dragged the mattress into the corridor and we waited. As soon as the rubbish man appeared, I leaned out of the window to witness the procedure. Up rattled the cart; out flew Anča with the mattress.

"I couldn't take it even if you gave me a gulden," he said, giving the horses the whip. "It's strictly forbidden."

"This is getting ridiculous," I said.

"It *is* ridiculous," she confirmed.

"Well then, come up with something, why don't you! Find out what other people do."

Off she flew. Within an hour she was back. "People say the thing to do is to burn it in the stove."

"Why, of course. How is it we didn't think of that? You know what? Find out whether anyone in the house needs a hot oven for making buns. Or wants to temper his stove. See what I mean?"

Off she flew once more. But no, no one was planning to make buns, no one needed a stove tempered. And she'd better be off to the market. She'd have no time to tend to the straw until evening. She couldn't sit around all day now, could she?

Well, so be it.

Evening came and we had our supper. Anča began twisting the straw into wisps and sticking them into the stove. I sat down at my desk, listening to the stove draw and crackle, puffing on my Virginia. I do love that stove-pipe drone.

Suddenly a racket rises up from the street: human voices, the house bell. I leap up and run into the corridor to see what the matter is. Apparently our chimney is spouting fire and it's spreading to the neighboring roofs.

"Stop, Anča! Stop, for heaven's sake! And quick! Drag the mattress back into the bedroom. If anyone knocks, you don't know a thing. Is the stove very hot?"

"From that couple of wisps? It'll cool down in no time."

No one knocked, thank God, and the fire stopped spreading. Soon people in the street had dispersed.

I stared up at the ceiling in great despair. And lay down again on the floor in great despair.

By morning, however, I had regained my spirits. I went right out and started investigating. I asked the policeman. I asked the porter. I asked all the women of my acquaintance.

The policeman saluted and said, "Can't say as I know." The porter raised his cap and said, "I really couldn't say." And my women friends said one after the other, "Yes, yes. It's always a problem."

"What are we going to do, Anča?" I said when I got home. "We can't leave it at this. You know how to make paper cones, don't you? Well then, I'll teach you. Watch."

Well, we made cone after cone and stuffed them with straw, and when we had a nice big pile of them I shoved a few into my pockets and went out for a stroll, strewing straw as I walked. That day I took six strolls. The next day twelve.

And so it went for four days, and still we had emptied only a tiny corner of the mattress. At that rate, I calculated, I was in for six months of strolls.

I need scarcely point out that I was as one obsessed: I could think of nothing else, see nothing else — my head was full of straw. In one corner of the room there were three trusses of straw, in another my poor depleted mattress, and in the middle the long sofa cushion. Where, where could I turn? Every night I so swore and cursed as I stretched out on the floor that I blush to think of it. I slept nary a wink and awoke before dawn to get an early start on my strolls.

It was in fact on one of those strolls that I noticed the jugs, milk cans, and baking pans my keen-sighted reader will remember from the beginning of the article. And this is how matters stand in Prague with jugs, milk cans, and baking pans.

Every Prague resident is entitled to have a jug or milk can and a baking pan as well. There is nothing in it, no penalty attached. But if the jug goes and breaks, then the fun begins! *What shall we do with it?*

Toss it into the courtyard and the caretaker will tell you to pick it up if you please. Toss it into the street and the policeman will pick you up. Toss it into the road sweeper's cart and the road sweeper will toss it back at you. Nor will even a generous gratuity do you any good: it's strictly forbidden. All right then. Take the jug out at night and, making certain you are unobserved, deposit it somewhere. Next day the road sweeper will pick it up free of charge, and there's an end to it.

I had a positively shameful idea. What if Anča and I took the mattress out at night, dragged it round the corner, and poured out all the straw. A nasty thought, a wicked thought, and illegal to boot, but I must admit it appealed to me. It's so easy to go bad.

But I have such bad luck. A policeman would appear out of nowhere and tell me to pick up the straw. I would stick to my guns, commit a crime of the tongue, whereupon I would be arrested, hauled off to jail — farewell, O spotless reputation! — but I would be past caring, I would . . .

"Excuse me, sir! Sir!" Anča cried, bursting into my room. "I know what to do with the straw! The milkwoman, the one who delivers to our street, she says she'd be glad to take it! She needs it at home for the cows! We can give it to her tomorrow!"

"Are you sure?"

"Positive!"

What else is there to say? I had a good night's sleep, and next morning Anča and I took the mattress down to the milkwoman. (Anča had made certain she would accept the gift.) It was a splendid moment. When the milkwoman handed me the empty mattress, I was so moved I kissed her hand and embraced her mare and set off for home with moist eyes.

Once there, we stuffed the mattress with the fresh straw, and when it was full I took hold of Anča and started whistling "O'er the Fresh Green Meadowland," and we stomped round the mattress till our heads spun.

Well, that is my story. That is what happened. Just as I've told it. It's a nice story, a timely story. I'm happy with it and so bring it to a close.

The Writer's Closing Prayer

"Heaven Almighty! I give thanks unto Thee for having protected my thoughts and guarded my witticisms from arousing the displeasure of the high and mighty, offending the sensibilities and moral purity of my fellow citizens, and harming the sales of tomorrow's paper, for it is the Sunday edition. Amen!"

Translated from the Czech by Michael Henry Heim

The Little Bulldog

Karel Pecka

SPRING DID NOT START TOO WELL for Malá Strana that year. The weather was more than foul and there was frost at night on and off right into the second fortnight of May. Heating had to be kept on and, what with increases in food prices, the old people had little to sing about. Then came the news of the Duchess's death. One evening she had not managed to hobble back to her hole in the house "At the Ass by the Cradle" and had remained lying in the passage. As ill luck would have it nobody had gone by the whole night and they had found her in the morning half-frozen. She had been a revolting figure at first glance, with the filth literally dropping off her. She used to shuffle up the street, step by painful step, wasting words on no one and returning no greeting. But she had been part of Malá Strana and her death was as momentous an event as if one of the old rickety houses had collapsed. With reprehensible hastiness, Mrs. Marie and Mrs. Marta from the house "At the Deep Cellar" fell in love. Retribution was swift, however, as they fell out of love just as quickly. Earlier, on account of the sharp winter frosts, the water mains had frozen up and, to repair the fault, a trench had been dug right across the road in front of the house "At the Broken Wheel." After completion of the inordinately lengthy repair, the hole had been carelessly filled in and the

From *Malá Strana Humoresques.*

earth had gradually subsided to form a rut deep enough to be a trench for a prone rifleman. The screech of brakes and the hollow thump of disintegrating shock absorbers rent the ears of the Neruda Street residents for more than a hundred yards in each direction. And the Tomcat pub had been closed, ostensibly for renovation. An uncustomary mood of irritability reigned in the remaining pubs where people would fly at each other on the slightest pretext. News filtered down from the Castle about further price increases, and there was no sign of warm sunny days on the horizon.

Take the day at the Two Suns pub, for instance, when Mr. Václav refused to let two soldiers from the Castle Guard sit at his table on the grounds that only locals were allowed to sit in the taproom, and anyway they were Slovaks. And indeed, the remaining seats were soon occupied. Mrs. Ela, who worked as a barmaid, came in. She had just discovered that during the winter the underside of her orange Renault had been damaged by rust. She was a slim, well-groomed lady who needlessly wore intellectual spectacles and whose succession of lovers over the previous years had consisted of painters at the very least. She was currently without a man friend, and this fact, combined with the poor state of business and these latest ravages of rust, put her in such a bad mood that she had decided not to go in to work; anyway, it was hardly worth the trouble for a few hundred measly crowns a shift. Shortly afterwards, Mr. Kadlus, the retired author, came in, followed, last of all, by the diminutive Bretschneider in his official suit with a bright modern tie.

"Oh, have they issued you with new ties?" Mrs. Ela greeted him unsmilingly.

"They're always issuing us with something," Bretschneider

agreed, equally morosely, and ordered a pack of Sparta filter cigarettes at their new price from Mrs. Margit at the counter.

"Give us one," Mr. Václav demanded.

"No, I don't intend to subsidize you. Bulldozer drivers get paid more than me," Bretschneider remarked curtly.

Mr. Václav was a jovial man of rotund appearance. After his usual dozen or so beers he would start to intone songs of every genre. He had a fairly unobtrusive voice and no one had ever objected to it — up to this last winter, that is. But just recently it had been suggested that he should keep quiet, and someone had even passed an insulting remark to the effect that he sounded like a dog howling. And to cap it all, Mr. Václav had been caught that day leaving work — as was his wont — at 10:30 in the morning and they had cut his bonus.

"Huh!" was his only response. "So tell us at least who's winning the Falklands War? And how come you're on the side of the Argentineans, seeing a fascist junta's in power there?"

"What do you mean by Falklands?" Bretschneider retorted. "They're the *Malvinas* Islands."

"Since when?" Mrs. Ela chimed in. "They were still the Falklands when it all started."

"You ask him over there," said Bretschneider, indicating Mr. Kadlus, the author. "His lot are a bunch of experts and philosophers. There's nothing they don't know."

"And what would you know about him?" Mrs. Ela said, frowning all the more. "You don't even know him."

"Who says I don't know him?" Bretschneider snapped back. "You'd be surprised what I know about him. We've got heaps of photos of his kind."

After that revelation, there was silence around the table until at last Mr. Václav spoke.

"Well, in my book that amounts to divulging official secrets. Hand over a cig and I won't divulge anywhere what you've just divulged."

"I won't," Bretschneider persisted. "I've already explained why, so the answer's no."

"Huh!" Mr. Václav barked in disgust. "I should have let those yokels sit here instead."

In the meantime, the two soldiers had drunk up their beer at the counter and were just about to leave. On overhearing that expression, however, they changed their minds.

"What's that you just said, you old wally?" interjected the smaller of them, a thick-set pugnacious type. "Who're you calling a yokel?"

"Look here, you just keep your hair on," Mr. Václav retorted. "You'd better buzz off back to your post before someone swipes the Castle."

"Hey, you," the taller one joined in, "I think you'd better step outside, mister."

"Why should I? I'm happy where I am. You're the one who's going out, mister. I don't like your company."

"Come on, you creep. You look like a yokel yourself."

"It occurs to me, Mr. Václav, that there is nothing for it but to answer the challenge from these gentlemen, unless you want to lose your last ounce of self-respect," said Mr. Kadlus, the author, intervening in the quarrel, and he placed his spectacles on the tabletop. "Allow me to accompany you."

"And what are you poking your nose in for?" the smaller soldier said, turning on him. "Something bothering you, or what?"

"There are lots of things that bother me," Mr. Kadlus replied with cold courtesy. "I can still remember a time when the Castle Guard was an elite corps made up of hand-picked men, all of them well-built and over six feet tall. When you had a giant like that standing either side of the main gate, it warmed the cockles of your heart. But nowadays they are obliged to give the present set of pygmies wooden crates to stand on. God knows where they manage to recruit such weedy fellows."

"Jesus Christ, what's that crap you're talking? So I'm a pygmy, am I?" the taller one yelled. "Outside, and we'll see who's a pygmy."

Mr. Kadlus, the author, stuck his two index fingers into his mouth to fish out his dentures, but at the critical moment Bretschneider intervened in his inimitable way. He rose out of his seat and, although he was on the small side, his voice rang out with authority, "That's enough. Clear out and make it snappy! Or I'll find some other way of dealing with you."

"Okay, okay," said the smaller one sullenly.

"He's the one that started on about yokels," the taller one said, pointing at Mr. Václav. "You heard him yourself."

In response Bretschneider pointed to the door: "Not another peep! And get off home before I book you."

The soldiers retreated and Bretschneider sat down again. He was just about to reach for his cigarettes to offer one to Mr. Václav, but before he could do so, Mrs. Ela remarked, "You really are a useless little backseat driver, aren't you? A proper little killjoy."

And the atmosphere was once more overtaken by the earlier sense of alienation. That was the way things were. And would go on being.

Mr. Roman occupied a spacious apartment in the house "At the Red Lamb." He had inherited it from his parents:

well-to-do Old Praguers who had crammed the apartment with furniture, carpets, and pictures, so that at one time it had given an impression of sepulchral gloom. Mr. Roman was a dapper fifty-year-old in the English manner. He had an oblong face with a well-trained mustache, slightly graying smoothly combed hair, and a slim build. He walked with a measured, leisurely gait and dressed with unassuming elegance. His scorn for the regime was such that he refused to listen to anti-government jokes and would set his watch by BBC broadcasts. To maintain his standard of living he was obliged now and then to sell a chest of drawers, an old candelabra, or a rare porcelain knickknack. But as the apartment emptied it became more beautiful; it brightened up and the remaining items of antique furniture began to breathe in the newly liberated space beneath the high stucco ceilings. Ladies of refined taste were happy to make visits there. And there was not one of them, in the commodious bathroom bedecked with polished mirrors, who did not feel tempted to view herself without clothes.

At the beginning of winter, Mr. Roman came by a new mistress. She was a lady at the age of transition from youth to maturity, when neither of those two attributes has lost its charm but rather, when the one outdoes the other and creates a unique kind of harmony. She had fair hair, a doll-like face with fine features, and a graceful figure with strikingly firm breasts. She was a splendid lover, adept in bed and bath, on the ground and in the air. There was only one thing she forbade Mr. Roman — a pupil and follower of the sage Vatsyayana's teachings — and that was when, borne on a wave of tenderness, he would express the desire to tattoo with his teeth on her creamy thighs "the line of points," "the coral and the jewel," and "the line of jewels," not to mention "the broken cloud." Thereupon, gently but firmly, she would always pull away his head with the caution, "No marks, darling, no marks, that's all!"

His mistress was married, you see, and had a family consisting of a husband — a nincompoop most likely — and two children. This circumstance affected their unique love life in two ways. Positively, in the sense that it foreordained a pure relationship untrammeled by needless chitchat and shilly-shallying: a brief quarter of an hour or twenty minutes over a glass of wine sufficed for them to free themselves from all encumbering garments and be ready for total mutual devotion. Equally unembellished was the culmination of their romps. After two hours of refined enjoyment, his mistress would sigh and declare it was time she was flying. Shortly afterward they would be walking side by side up Neruda Street. And now would come the negative aspect referred to: the bleakest moments of an otherwise splendid evening. His mistress lived somewhere out in Břevnov, and like a diligent wife and mother she would always arrive with shopping for her family, and Mr. Roman was a gentleman. And thus, while she was cataloging little Jeník's measles and young Maruška's problems at school, Mr. Roman would be humping a capacious shopping bag full of meat, flour, and other confoundedly heavy goods. The worst stretch of the journey still lay ahead in the form of the precipitous Town Hall Steps, as unrelenting as the ascent to Mount Sněžka. At this point Mr. Roman would always wonder whether it might be infra dig to take a rucksack with him on this hike next time. With the steps conquered, the last section to Pohořelec Square was not too bad, and once he had laid down his burden at the tram stop his capacity for refined conversation would gradually return. From that moment on things got better and better. The mistress would depart and Mr. Roman would retrace his steps. And as the most strenuous effort reaps the sweetest rewards, the moment he reached those very same Town Hall Steps and the vista of that magical street opened up below him, he felt a well-deserved sense of being requited with his fate, nay, more — a deep inner calm, achieved at the cost of superhuman effort.

One evening he was heading thus homewards with his long, easy stride and was actually whistling, as if the prevailing Malá Strana depression had somehow passed him by. Approaching Dittrich's pharmacy, he saw from a distance Mr. Motejl sitting on the low wall that runs parallel to the steps of St. John's Hill, his flower-patterned jug of beer at his side. He knew Mr. Motejl by sight as a neighbor, naturally, although it seemed odd to him that he should be sitting out there on a cold wall on such a chilly evening, and in his slippers. As he reached the illuminated clock a little further down the street, he noticed that Mr. Jaromil was just leaving the Bonaparte pub with yet another girl. But that also was no concern of his. He walked calmly on until all at once he was taken aback by the sound of high-pitched female screaming mingled with an irate man's voice and dull thuds, like someone beating a kettle drum. He turned round and saw Mr. Motejl laying into Mr. Jaromil, who was splayed up against the wall. Mr. Motejl was yelling something to the effect that he wasn't going to put up with that sort of hanky-panky any more. Mr. Jaromil was taking blows to the chest and solar plexus. Without offering any resistance, he slipped to his knees on the pavement. Mr. Roman watched the spectacle for several moments, aware that there was something comical about it, before crossing the street to intervene in some way. Mr. Motejl, wrongly thinking that he had won and that his opponent had had enough, interrupted his activity for a split second. Mr. Jaromil seized the opportunity and, pulling himself together, landed a phenomenal uppercut straight to Mr. Motejl's shaggy jaw. It was such an accurate and crushing blow that it lifted Mr. Motejl right out of his slippers, which remained standing neatly side by side on the pavement while their owner was knocked backward into the middle of the street.

"Enough's enough, gentlemen," Mr. Roman said, placing himself between the rivals. "Call it quits."

After the straight jab he had received, Mr. Motejl seemed inclined to accept a truce. But not so Mr. Jaromil.

"Not on your life," he roared. "He waylaid me from round the corner like some Dick Turpin. You saw for yourself."

With these words he stepped round Mr. Roman and with another punch sent his opponent flying back to his slippers. Mr. Motejl put them back on and was staggering toward the steps when he received a third blow that sent him hurtling over the lower wall where he had been sitting earlier. "That's enough now, sir," Mr. Roman repeated. "The account is settled."

"Yes, I think you're right," Mr. Jaromil agreed this time, but in a final burst of bellicosity grabbed the flower-patterned jug that was still standing on the wall and poured its contents over the head of Mr. Motejl who was feebly picking himself up from the cobbles on the other side.

That event caused Mr. Motejl's never-more-than-scant prestige to plummet to near zero. The fact that he was an unsociable, crabby individual who enjoyed backbiting worthy citizens — something he did with unconcealed malice and a knowing undertone when he had had a few beers — and that he was always the unconstructive sort of customer that one finds in every pub when all is said and done, these were things that Malá Strana people were prepared to tolerate. But waylaying a table companion — ambushing him in fact — that smacked of jungle law and went against the unwritten rules of good neighborliness and any sort of decent behavior. And so from that evening onward, Mr. Motejl would sit boycotted at the Bonaparte in his chair by the kitchen door; nobody would waste words on him, and, aware of his moral trouncing, he sunk into an even deeper gloom bordering on despair. And it was compounded by the banefully dismal mood which then prevailed, when it seemed there was no escaping the general malaise and that things would stay that way forever.

And then suddenly, from one day to the next, spring invaded Malá Strana. And it happened to be just when the mid-May cold snap was expected, as if to prove how everything was topsy-turvy and up the spout. Liberated from the frost, the forsythia shot forth its flames, the chestnut-tree buds rushed to make up for lost time, and even the cagey acacia started to look restless somehow. The change affected people in a similarly beneficent manner, smoothing frown lines from faces and injecting souls with optimism.

In the taproom at the Bonaparte, which opens onto the street and is reserved for the permanent inhabitants of the quarter, several of the regulars were seated around the tables in convivial chat. Mrs. Ela was telling Mr. Kadlus that she was going into work again now and then and that it looked as if something could be done with the car after all. Mr. Jeřábek was predicting the course of the next soccer World

Cup and his adversaries were expressing their views in a moderate fashion, without raising voices or indulging in personal invective. When Bretschneider declared that our team would reach the final he was neither pilloried nor expelled from the company. Instead a sigh was heard, "It's quite possible, gentlemen. Anything is possible nowadays." And the author of this rejoinder was none other than Mr. Roman.

Mr. Milan was drawing the pints with panache. He turned the taps like an organ virtuoso, and the beer left perfect rings down the glasses as it was drunk. The din of youngsters from the bars at the rear sounded more muffled, almost peaceable. A tone of affability actually entered the voice of Mr. Rippl, the landlord, and he even cracked a joke from time to time. Only Mr. Motejl sat like a sourpuss, neither taking part in the conversation nor being invited to.

The calm of early evening wafted in from the street through the open door and a procession of gauzily-clad beauties, newly emerged from their winter pupae, would saunter across the drinkers' field of vision.

There are moments that occur in company like the incident in *Sleeping Beauty:* all motion comes to a halt for several seconds and the conversation dies. Once upon a time the phenomenon was known as "an angel flying by." Well, that evening the angel chose the Bonaparte. Into a situation akin to mass catalepsy, a dog entered the taproom. It walked straight up the two steps from the street as if it felt itself to be a valued regular. The eyes of everyone present were suddenly fixed on it and the little dog wagged its stump of a tail in greeting. It then licked its chops and sat down on the floor, surveying the company. It was a French bulldog with a salt-and-pepper coloring. Enormous eyes shone out of its genial face and its expression was so guileless and trusting that not even the state executioner would have had the heart to kick it. It was a creature that physically emanated goodness and instantly won general sympathy. The gaze of the regulars, expecting the arrival of the dog's owner, immediately switched to the doorway. But since none appeared, their gaze returned to the diminutive dog, then back to the doorway, and back again, as though they were watching a tennis match. Even Mr. Jaromil, seated on the bench by the stove with a brand-new girl, interrupted his billing and cooing momentarily to see what was up.

The landlord, Mr. Rippl, was a dog breeder and got on better with dogs than with many people. He now stepped forward, bent down, scratched the bulldog behind the ear and boomed out feelingly, "Well, where's your master then, boy?"

Then he went out into the street, returning a moment later to announce to the still silent company, "There's no one there. I couldn't see anyone the animal might belong to."

Bulldogs are a singular race of dogs. At first sight the classic boxer, with its athletic, muscular frame on nervous legs, arouses respect on account of some strange hidden power. That first impression is tempered by the appearance of its muzzle; the observer is at a loss what to make of its expression: half threatening, half comical. French bulldogs, however, with their diminutive frame, do not inspire any fear. But this one was not even funny. It had a serious and dignified face, and whenever it gave someone one of its direct, attentive, and lingering looks, it was as if it were saying, "I am observing you and registering the fact that you are definitely a good fellow. And therefore I trust you." Noblesse oblige, the dog was a noble creature and from the very first had the entire pub on its side.

But it must belong to someone, mustn't it? Surely nobody could be such a brute as to abandon a dog like that, people began to say.

"Oho, don't you believe it, gentlemen. People are real pigs," Mr. Rippl growled. "When the price of the dog license went up, you could see dogs tied to trees in the woods. Or some jerk would go into a telephone booth and leave the dog there. Just look at this one: he's got no tag on his collar."

"I bet he ran off and his master's looking for him," someone remarked. "I saw one just like that on Malá Strana Square, but I didn't recognize the lady walking with it."

"And I, when I was out walking just recently, caught sight of a specimen like it at the top of Neruda Street, by the bend toward the Castle," Mr. Kadlus, the writer, observed.

"Let's wait and see. Someone's sure to come and fetch him," Mr. Jeřábek suggested.

Mrs. Alena appeared in the kitchen doorway and came over to the bulldog. She stroked it and declared lovingly, "Ah, isn't he a lovely boy. You come with me, I've got something nice for you."

The bulldog accepted the invitation with exemplary manners. It expressed its gratitude by licking its flat face, getting up, and slowly following Mrs. Alena into the kitchen. There was not the slightest trace of servility in its behavior. Returning from its supper, it did the rounds of the two tables in the taproom and ceremoniously greeted the locals one by one, in well-bred recognition of its acceptance into the inner circle. Then it set off on a tour of inspection of the rear bars, crammed with the long-haired Hashemites and their little girlfriends. The tumult from there was like Niagara Falls from fairly close up, but the little dog pattered into that pandemonium with not a sign of fear. It couldn't come to any harm, could it, seeing that everyone was so nice.

Mr. Pepa, the potman, arrived from the back with a whole lot of empty glasses and set them down on the counter. He took a tin of snuff out of the pocket of his white jacket and had a pinch. "That dog's getting under my feet. What's to be done with him?"

He said this as if into thin air, but everyone knew the question was directed at the landlord, Mr. Rippl, who was a dictator when it came to deciding how the pub was to be run. However, Mr. Rippl was standing with his coccyx perched on the counter, silently contemplating the portrait of General Bonaparte, his great predecessor, hung on the wall opposite. Mr. Pepa was a tough card or he would never have stood the course under those conditions. He could carry a dozen beers in his mighty fists, which were also used on occasions for calming hot-blooded customers in the back rooms.

"For crying out loud," he lamented, and not having waited for any answer, grasped only ten beers this time to be on the safe side and set off with them.

Now raised, the question remained hanging in the air. Yes, that's a fact, what's to be done with the dog if nobody comes to collect it? Where's it to go, wondered each of those present, stealing glances at each other. At that moment the little bulldog strolled back into the taproom, sat down in front of the bar and scratched itself thoughtfully behind its ear. Presently Mr. Pepa rushed in with some empty glasses and almost fell over it. He deposited the glasses noisily in the sink and went to stand beside Mr. Rippl, who was still glued to the counter.

"I'm telling you he's a bloody idiot," he declared, adding after a short pause, "and I'll prove it to you."

He went over to the resting bulldog, leaned over it and said, "Well, what d'you say? You are a bloody idiot, aren't you?"

The little bulldog turned his deeply human gaze on Mr. Pepa, stood up, and wagged his stump of a tail.

"And who isn't a bloody idiot, when all is said and done?" whispered Mr. Roman.

"There's a good idiot," Mr. Pepa said, patting the dog's angular head. Then he stood up and walked toward the door. "Here boy, here boy," he coaxed him, and when the dog started to follow him, he suddenly pointed to the street, "And now buzz off home! You've had a great time, but you're in the way, and enough's enough, you bloody idiot. Buzz off home!"

And the bulldog did as it was bid. Taking its time, it walked down the steps and without a backward glance disappeared from sight.

"And that's that," Mr. Pepa said, turning round and going over to join Mr. Rippl leaning against the counter. "Well, he really was getting under people's feet, wasn't he?"

But his statement evoked nothing but silence. Such unaccustomed lengthy silence in the taproom brought Mrs. Alena scurrying out of the kitchen to see what was up.

"Where's he gone? What've you done with him?" she demanded, her voice getting louder all the time. And when the silence continued, she rushed over to the pub door screaming, "How could you? Haven't you got any feelings at all?"

A moment later Mr. Rippl shifted from his spot and muttered, "Anyone waiting to pay at the back there? I'll do the rounds."

"After all," Bretschneider added, "an intelligent dog like that ought to be able to find its way home."

"Bulldogs are very intelligent creatures," said Mrs. Ela. "I had a bulldog during my second marriage, but it was an ordinary boxer. Or was it during the third one? Anyway, he was the nicest one, that one with the dog."

But before the conversation got under way again, Mrs. Alena was standing in the doorway holding the little bulldog in her arms. She set it down on the floor and announced, "He almost got run over by a car. Just let someone try and harm him, that's all."

With her bosom held proudly high she crossed to the kitchen, followed by the bulldog. It was not offended and still had its wise, artless expression. People are good, after all, why should they harm me one way or another? Its stay in the kitchen was brief, however. Presently, it reappeared in the taproom and with it the earlier quandary.

"How about you taking him, Fanda?" Mr. Pepa asked Mr. Rippl. He was relaxing while waiting for Mr. Milan to top off a line of beers. "You keep dogs, don't you?"

"I've got Alsatians, two of them," said Mr. Rippl, "and they'd wolf him down after dinner for dessert."

"And what about our author?" said Mrs. Ela, trying her neighbor. "There you are, vegetating all on your own, without a woman. You must be awfully lonely and miserable. A little dog like that would cheer you up no end."

"I was interrogated by the secret police over every one of my books, which is why I laid down my pen," said Mr. Kadlus, pushing his spectacles back on his nose. "That dog is more dangerous than a man-eating Bengal tiger. Observe, Mrs. Ela, how through its very character, conduct, and behavior it awakens a sense of responsibility in people, how it encourages the better side of their nature. It's a terrorist of a dog, and if I'm not wrong in my assessment of that creature, it would most likely induce me to start writing again. But it is my intention to end my days in peace and quiet and not behind bars."

Mr. Václav and Mr. Eman came tottering into the taproom on unsteady legs. Mr. Eman, the white-haired waiter from "At the Swan," stared at the little bulldog and said, "What's Prince doing here? Surely Mr. Pulec is not back on the drink again!"

"Do you know the dog, Eman?" Mrs. Ela asked skeptically. The others also silently harbored doubts that the solution to the mystery could be so banal.

"Of course I do. It must be Prince," Mr. Eman maintained, addressing the dog directly by that name, and when the little bulldog raised its head and nestled up to his legs, he started to stroke its back. "And where's his master?"

"He came in alone. Perhaps he got lost."

"It doesn't matter, I'll take him home to Mr. Pulec. He might be out searching for him all over the place," said Mr. Eman, catching the dog up into his arms and tottering out.

A sense of relief irradiated the taproom. They all drank up their beer with a smile and Mr. Milan was again turning the taps with the deftness of a juggler. And the relief gave way to joy when Mr. Eman returned and announced, "Mr. Pulec wasn't in; I expect he's out looking for Prince. So I left him with the neighbors."

The good cheer which then pervaded the taproom in the Bonaparte pub was almost tangible. Alas, it was short-lived. Half an hour later a man burst in, dragging behind him on separate leashes two French bulldogs. And at first sight one would have said they were from the same litter.

"This isn't Prince," he said, going over to Mr. Eman and pressing one of the leashes into his palm. "Take a look: my Prince has a white front."

A chill ran through the room. The general consternation was summed up succinctly by Mr. Pepa. "For crying out loud," he said.

"But that one also answered to the name of Prince," Bretschneider objected, pointing to the dog without the white front.

"I think I ought to recognize my own dog," scowled the newcomer.

"Look here, Mr. Pulec, since you've got one already, couldn't you, er . . . ," Mr. Eman stammered.

"No," Mr. Pulec refused curtly. Then he turned on his heel and departed without a word of farewell, dragging his Prince behind him on the leash. A moment later he stuck his head back in the door and added, "I left him my own leash: it's brand new."

"What a brute! What a bloody ogre!" yelped Mrs. Alena from the kitchen. She had gone weak at the knees and had to lean on the door frame for support.

"What sort of decency can one expect from reformed alcoholics?" Mr. Kadlus uttered with vexation. "To a man they are schizophrenic sissies who have lost all courage and self-esteem, and also, therefore, any dignity, any future, any raison d'être."

But the enduring dog was back again like an embodied dilemma. The mood of tension was too much for Mr. Jaromil's new fiancée. She had the look of a sociologist: flat-chested and wearing large round spectacles with dark lenses.

"Jaromil, how about you taking it in?"

"Me?" Mr. Jaromil ejaculated.

"Yes, you. You're on your own and you're bored and so you go out looking for various kinds of adventures. That dog would give you something to do, something else to think about. It would even act as a watchdog."

"For heaven's sake, there's hardly room in my little apartment for myself," Mr. Jaromil protested in horror. "With two people there it's so cramped that movement is limited to the minimum."

"That's because the entire apartment is taken up by one enormous bed. If you were to cut a bit off it, it would show more consideration, and not just toward visitors," the young lady said, undeterred. "And talk about a bit, you could easily get rid of half of it."

"Wh-a-at? Saw a lump off my bed?" Mr. Jaromil was getting hot under the collar. "Never. It'd be like portioning my own flesh."

The resolute tone of the last sentence threatened to provoke a serious lover's tiff. But at the last moment, when the young woman was opening her mouth in preparation for a bayonet charge, Mr. Motejl, hitherto sullenly silent, intervened. He rose from his seat, went over to Mr. Eman, and gently took the leash from his quavering hands. "I'll take him home, until someone comes to claim him," he said and returned to his seat, taking Prince with him.

"And what if no one does?" Bretschneider broke the ensuing silence with the question that was on the lips of every member of the company.

"Then he'll stay with me for good," Mr. Motejl uttered in strangled tones, as if taking a solemn oath. "That is, unless there are any objections."

"Well, for that you deserve . . ." Mr. Rippl smiled and it seemed as if he would say, "a double," but he stopped himself in time. "You deserve a medal."

At closing time, Mr. Motejl left the pub with his old flower-patterned jug and his new Prince. A chance witness who met him that night later swore solemnly that he had heard him humming softly to himself.

The little bulldog was taken for a walk the next day by its happy owner. But more important, Mr. Motejl had rehabilitated himself and was accepted once more as a full and equal member of the neighborhood.

That was the moment too when spring at last took over the government of the community in accordance with the unalterable laws which state that every winter, however long, must end one day, and that when December's past and gone, May is finally on its way.

Prague, May 1982
Translated from the Czech by A. G. Brain

American Heating, Josef Vrkoč, Vinohrady

Jindřiška Smetanová

I WAS BRINGING A CHAIR HOME from the carpenter — it had a cherrywood back and striped upholstery and had just been repaired — when I saw a woman walking in front of me in an eccentric checkered dress and a raincoat, with a movie camera and a portable Japanese tape recorder slung around her neck.

She stopped by the wall surrounding the Maltese Garden and filmed a pump with a sign on it saying: THIS WATER IS HARMFUL TO YOUR HEALTH. Then she recorded the sound of the creaky handle and the splashing water. A hundred meters on she was entranced by the mill wheel, so she filmed it too and recorded the slapping of its paddles in the water.

"Oh, how marvelous," she cried upon entering a small courtyard near the mill and seeing a live hen. She filmed the hen and recorded its clucking, along with the sounds of people kneeling in the nearby Church of the Virgin Mary.

Then she saw me. She filmed me with the chair and asked if I would sit down on it. She spoke the Czech our countrymen who live in America speak.

"A little bit to the left," she requested. "I'd like to get the Church of St. Nicholas and Hradčany behind you and that chicken in front of you. And don't look so sad. Smile. It'll be a lovely shot."

She pointed to the paving stones and then to the church

tower, the rooftops, and the chimneys and kept repeating enthusiastically, "How splendid, how marvelous!"

"I beg your pardon," she apologized, and introduced herself as Evelyn Nowak.

Her father had moved to America in 1906, she said. "He was a professor of philosophy and he understood everything except business. The poor man had to shoot himself. But Mother didn't know anything except how to bake wonderful strudel, so we got rich."

She offered me a Chesterfield and asked if I would let her rest a while in the chair.

"How perfectly beautiful," she said, looking around the square. "I collect antiques," she explained. "And you?"

"I collect antiques too," I said without thinking. "So does my husband. He's crazy about chairs. Last year alone he's brought home seven. Six of them were the same — cane Thenetka chairs from the end of the last century. He claimed they could have had furniture like that in the dining room of the Titanic and I never stopped believing that our chairs had survived the disaster. But the moment one sat on them they collapsed."

"I'm so sorry," she said, "but most antiques are like that."

She wanted to know what I collected. Pictures? Furniture?

"Everything," I said. "Pictures, furniture, small objets d'art. But I also collect architecture, monuments, and sometimes even people. I don't like collections that are confined to a room, or even to a display case. If an antique is really rare and noble, it needs space and a natural setting."

Evelyn Nowak from Texas was beside herself with curiosity.

"Would you show me your collection?"

"By all means," I said. "We can begin at once."

I picked up the chair and took the collector to 9 Lazeňská

Street. "First of all, please sit down while I say a few words," I told her. "Everything that goes into my collection is absolutely genuine. There are no imitations."

"That's very important," she declared, "because more imitations are bought and sold today than ever before in the history of antique collecting. People have gone crazy. Everyone wants to have at least one inventoried item from the imperial treasury. My brother has a factory that makes antique furniture," she confessed. "He makes everything from ancient Egyptian thrones and Ludwig the Great bedroom suites to colonial sideboards."

This was not nice.

"You'll probably be all the more interested in this door handle then," I said, pointing at the big wooden door to number nine.

The handle was shaped like a paw, as though a slender and playful kitten on the other side of the door were reaching her foot through the hole. For a good two hundred years, everyone going in and out pressed his hand on the wrought iron paw to open the door or close it, and those thousands of hands removed minute fragments of the rough surface, leaving behind an equally minute portion of their own warmth and the touch of living skin.

The paw had lost its metallic qualities but in return had gained a soul.

"It's absolutely precious," whispered Mrs. Evelyn Nowak from Texas. "My brother would give half his fortune for such a handle."

Unfortunately the handle was not for sale.

"Thirty-nine people live in this building. Each day they leave and come back and they're constantly stroking the handle, so its value as a collector's item keeps on growing. But that would stop the moment you took it back to Texas. It would lose its satin softness and its chocolate shading. If your brother spent half his fortune on it, he'd go out of business. He'd have to mount it on another door and then he'd have to walk in and out of that door all day long for the rest of his life, because there is only one motion that can maintain the formal perfection of the handle: pressure from the top down and then a half circle to the left. You can't use polish to keep it smooth either, the way you could a brass mortar and pestle or a coffee mill. The rarity of this handle comes from the light, saline dampness of the human hand."

"Oh, that's too bad," said Mrs. Evelyn Nowak. She got up from the chair, filmed the handle, and then recorded the sound of the door opening. She couldn't get enough of it.

"Can you show me more from your magnificent collection?"

"Of course."

I took my chair and led the collector onto the Charles Bridge, to the two bollards by the staircase leading down to Kampa.

She delicately caressed the surface of the stone pillars with the ends of her fingers.

"Magnificent polished pink marble," she sighed blissfully.

"Yes, people have polished it with their bare hands. Now watch. Everyone who goes down the stairs will touch the bollard with a circular movement of their hand. Some things you never notice, but these two columns of stone have a magic power of attraction. You can't pass by without stroking them."

For a while we watched. A child walked by, stopped at one of the bollards, and ran his index finger over its shiny round head. Then a gentleman turned toward the stairs and he too absently caressed the pastel softness of the Slivenec marble. Mrs. Evelyn Nowak from Texas filmed them both.

"Oh," she said longingly, "I'd love to have these columns at the foot of the staircase in my garden. I'm fascinated by stone that's been polished by the touch of human skin. In Padua I stood for hours in front of St. Anthony's tombstone. Women who want children have kissed the marble so often they've made a deep depression in it."

I shook my head. "These bollards, like the tombstone of Anthony of Padua, can't be bought and taken somewhere else. You would spoil them, Mrs. Nowak. They would turn rough, because to keep them this smooth, they need the pressure of two or three hundred thousand hands a year. In your garden, the rain would damage them and bad weather would crumble them. I only collect objects that can't be bought and taken away."

I felt I had to convince her. "Are you afraid of heights?"

"Not at all," she said.

First we walked down the stairs and across Kampa, then past the mill wheel again and through a remarkable portal in the style of the Czech renaissance.

Climbing a wooden staircase, we came to a loft and then went up a little set of stairs, apparently fashioned for chickens, to the first attic, and above that to the second.

Carrying the chair all the way up was a complicated business, but I needed the chair to show Evelyn Nowak from Texas some more of my collection.

"Now if you'll just be patient," I said, "I first have to position this chair exactly so the picture you will see through the attic window will be unforgettable. If I put it in the wrong place, all you will see will be a very forgettable piece of sky and a leaky gutter."

At last the chair was in exactly the right place. "Please sit down," I said.

The collector sat down.

Through the round gable window she saw a quiet grove of chimneys stretching out before her, suspended in the October afternoon. It had a veil of wild grape draped across it; a Balkan dove sat on its brow and behind its ear was an abandoned nest.

"What a moving picture," she whispered. "I've never seen a more beautiful illustration to Baudelaire."

She filmed the view from the gable window and recorded the throaty gurgling of the dove. Before we left the attic she wanted to take a look around, so she crawled under the low beams and, her hat full of cobwebs, she suddenly stopped and pointed to a dark corner where there was an old abandoned potbellied stove with little mica windows in the door and a chrome-plated handle like a diadem. A small metal plate affixed to its breast bore the words: AMERICAN HEATING, JOSEF VRKOČ, VINOHRADY.

"Why have you been keeping this a secret?" Evelyn admonished me.

"Because it's not part of my collection. The stove belongs to a neighbor of mine. She put it up here shortly after 1945. But I'll tell you its story if you're interested."

She sat down in the chair in front of the stove.

"When the war was over, the allied troops held a parade in Prague," I began. "An elite unit of Patton's army drove in from Pilsen to take part. A distant relative of our neighbor served in the unit, and he came to visit his great aunt with several of his buddies. It was autumn, and when five men of the U.S. Army walked into the living room, the stove was lit and the glowing coke shone through the mica windows and illuminated the plate that said AMERICAN HEATING, JOSEF VRKOČ, VINOHRADY. The family reunion ended about midnight with five pie-eyed sergeants standing at attention in front of the stove, crying and singing the American national anthem."

"I must have this stove," said Evelyn Nowak of Texas, wiping away her tears. And then with the same handkerchief she dusted off the stove.

"It's yours. The woman it belonged to has been dead for a long time. But I can't imagine what use you'll put it to in Texas. It makes a lot of dust and ashes."

She looked at me in amazement. "Why should I use it for heating, darling? I have the best air-conditioning money can buy — all built in. But my brother, who makes antiques, will install a red light in the stove and a stereo recording of burning coke. Have you any idea what an American Heating stove from Czechoslovakia will mean to my family? My goodness!"

On Malá Strana Square she danced into a taxi in her high heels and the same day she took the stove away, probably to Texas.

All she left me was a memory, and the undying hope that one day someone in a group of Czech tourists traveling through Texas would decide to visit a distant aunt on his mother's side — a certain Mrs. Evelyn Nowak — and at midnight the collector would take her guests into the salon, press a button, and the little mica windows in the stove with the plate bearing the words AMERICAN HEATING, JOSEF VRKOČ, VINOHRADY would light up with a warm glow and they would hear the sounds of burning coke in stereo. At a moment like that, only a cynic would be ashamed to cry and sing "Where is My Homeland?"

Translated from the Czech by Paul Wilson

The Sword of St. Wenceslas

František Langer

THE MOST BEAUTIFUL of Prague's seven bridges — the most beautiful bridge in the world, in fact — is the Charles Bridge. It is six centuries old, and each century has endowed it with something of beauty. One saw the building of the double fortified gate on the Malá Strana side, standing like a shield to defend the heart of Prague. During another, it was given the ornamental tower at the Old Town end, a tower decked with stone tracery and tassels and fringes, like a baldachin over the entrance to a ceremonial hall. In later ages still, it sprouted two rows of statuary stretching the length of the bridge and transforming it into a Royal Way that arches over the Vltava and the city. But every age endowed it as well with a piece of history, a story or legend, so that as you walk across the bridge, it speaks to you like a chronicle in stone, and the sound of each footfall is like a line from that history.

The most famous tale of all is the one about the miraculous sword. That sword, so the story goes, is immured in the bridge, though no one knows where. But when things are at their worst in Bohemia, St. Wenceslas will ride forth at the head of the Knights of Blaník to save his land. When he reaches the bridge, his horse will stumble on a stone and the stone will be overturned, revealing beneath it the famous sword. Grasping it, St. Wenceslas will brandish it over his head three times and cry aloud: "Off with the heads of all our foes!" And instantly, all the enemies of the Czech lands will find themselves shorter by a head, and peace and tranquillity will reign once more in Bohemia, for ever and ever.

It is an age-old legend and whenever times have been hard — and that has been often enough — every fiber of our being has yearned for the prophecy to be fulfilled. But the time has never yet been ripe, not even when we thought things were as bad as they could possibly get.

It was in 1939 when, as you know, Hitler's Germans — soldiers, policemen, and cut-throats — occupied our lands, murdering, jailing, and plundering us and taking away our rights and freedoms and, along with them, our memory of the past and our hope for the future, not to mention our language — the very breath of the nation. It was a time of despair and desolation, and we lived in terror of the future.

Then, during the first Christmas of those dark days, something happened that changed the way the legend will be told in the future. So listen, children! This concerns you.

At that time, the Christmas season brought the unhappy people some consolation and strength, for they were able to get together more easily than at other times. For what could have been more welcome than to feel a true Czech heart beating close to your own? And so the churches of Prague were full for the Christmas midnight mass that year, and the fullest of all, packed to the doors, was the grand cathedral of St. Vitus. People thronged in from every corner of Prague, but unlike other years, the parents, as if in collusion with each other, brought their older children along with them. They had not conspired to do so, they were simply all driven by the same idea: "What if the Germans ban our ancient midnight ceremony next year? They've banned everything else we're proud of, everything that sustains us. The midnight mass at

St. Vitus is held over the tombs of our kings, and we sing our own hymns. The beauty and the history of the place, and the sanctity of the moment, will awaken proud thoughts of our past and strengthen our belief in a future rebirth — the very thoughts our conquerors wish to extinguish from our hearts and minds. Let us take our children with us, and if this is to be the last time, they will have something to remember all of their days."

As people left the cathedral after midnight, snow was falling, real Christmas snow — thick and dry and clean, as if someone were emptying feather pillows out in heaven. There was not a breath of wind, and the snow fell silently and settled like the softest down. Streets and staircases were sprinkled with sugar, every balustrade and every bollard was piled high with the whitest whipped cream, the towers were like sugar loaves and the roofs of Malá Strana like iced cakes. Statues donned white coats, ermine fringes, and swan-like robes, like fairies, spirits, and princesses. Snow squirrels, snow doves, and snow cats slept on all the window ledges and cornices, on all the bare tree branches. It was a true fairy-tale city, but then you all know the magical splendor of Prague when it is bedecked with snow.

The children, I hardly need tell you, did not keep to the sidewalks like their parents, but set off down the middle of the street, wading through the falling snow. In their hundreds and thousands they trailed through the streets of Malá Strana and then under the Bridge Tower until they reached the Charles Bridge. And there, as they were passing Kampa Island, the biggest lads, the ones who were walking in front — Jenda, Toník, Ferda, Pepík, Pavel, and some others — caught sight of something. Right in the middle of the bridge, by the statue of Bruncvík, there was a bare, snowless patch, and in the middle of that patch, something glistened and shone like a white flame or a flash of silver.

One of the lads picked the mysterious object up. It was a big, beautiful sword with a silver haft and a scabbard set with sparkling jewels and it gleamed so brightly that if it hadn't been so heavy you might have thought you were holding rays of sunlight or moonbeams. The boys knew at once what they had found, and the news spread quickly to those at the back, the slowpokes who had not yet arrived at the bridge. For what else could it possibly be but the famed sword of the legend?

The first thing, of course, was to hide the sword from prying eyes, because even on that fairy-tale night Prague was teeming with German patrols who strutted along the Prague streets in twos and fours in their helmets and long greatcoats, with revolvers in their belts and rifles over their shoulders. But it wouldn't be a proper fairy tale without evil spirits or monsters, would it? And so under an overcoat it went. And when it became too heavy for Vašek, Jarouš carried it a way, and then Matouš, and some of the girls hid it under their fur coats for a while too. So the children spirited the sword away right under the Germans' noses.

Before they set off home, word had spread among the children that they were all to meet at Kampa Island the next morning at eleven o'clock underneath the stone bridge, just by the statue of Bruncvík.

On Christmas day in the morning, all (and if not all, then almost all) the children of Prague rushed to Kampa. Kampa is an island between the wide arm of the Vltava River and the narrow Čertovka Stream. A flight of steps runs down from the Charles Bridge to a small square that is famous for the potters' markets held there four times a year and the acacia trees that bloom there once a year and fill the air with their heady scent. There the children assembled. It was the biggest gathering of children Prague had ever seen, but since they were only children, the German police took no notice. "They are no concern of ours," they thought, "and we have nothing to fear from them." Had they but known . . . but they didn't, that's the main thing.

The wintry Christmas sun smiled down, and while they were waiting the children threw snowballs at each other, pushed snow down each other's collars, called each other names, cavorted and kicked up a din, and the time just flew by. At eleven o'clock, a young lad — Frantík, Standa, or Vlád'a, I don't know which — vaulted up onto the steps leading to the bridge so that everyone could see him. When he raised the magic sword above his head all the children fell silent and doffed their caps, bonnets, berets, and fur hats. Then the young lad said, "Listen, everyone. Yesterday we found this famous sword, the one there are so many stories about. Now we have to decide what to do with it."

It was a big question, but the answers started flying right back. They ought to hand the sword over to their parents, or to the school, and some wise person proposed that it was a valuable relic and ought to be taken to the museum for safe-keeping. But then another lad got up, the sort of fellow who doesn't have much to say for himself as a rule, but knows how to get on with the job when the time arrives. And he said, "I think we should do what it says in the legend: unsheathe it and say the proper words. The Germans' heads will roll and we'll have peace and tranquillity in the Czech lands once and for all." Then he heaved a sigh of relief.

All the children shouted, "Yes! You're right! Hear, hear! Hooray! Go to it, Pepík" (or Mirek or Jenda, or whatever his name was), and by this time the lad had the sword in his hands (because as I said, he was the sort of fellow who didn't waste words) but try as he might, he couldn't unsheathe the sword. Then the other boys tried, including a number of tough, muscular youths, but no one could pull it out. The sword seemed welded in its scabbard.

Then another young fellow jumped up. He was somewhat on the small side, so he had to wave his thin arms in the air for a long time before the others noticed him. "Listen," he said, "Doesn't the prophecy say that St. Wenceslas himself will draw the sword when things are at their worst in Bohemia? So how can we children hope to do it? But the question is, how come it was lying in our path last night, just like a Christmas present? I think it's because the sword isn't safe in the Charles Bridge any more. When the Germans read our chronicles and find out it's hidden there, they'll search the bridge from end to end. They'll even tear it down and take it apart just to rob the Czechs of their magic weapon. So I think the sword has been given to us children for safekeeping. One of us should take it and hide it, and if they feel any sort of danger, they'll pass it along to someone else. No one needs to know where it is, but we'll all take care of it. The sword will be safer with us than it would be in a lifeless piece of stone. That way, it'll survive until St. Wenceslas comes with the Knights of Blaník to rescue us."

All the children knew he was right and they all turned to look at the sword. Suddenly, it seemed to come alive. It glowed and pulsated like frozen fire and sent forth dazzling rays that danced about the children's heads, as if caressing them for their determination. It was a glorious moment: none of the children made a sound. And in the silence, the striking of the St. Nicholas clock descended through the clean winter air. Then the noonday bells began to ring at the Theatine monastery, at St. Thomas' and St. Vitus', and over the river at the Knights of the Cross, the Týn Church, and St. James, and from even further away at Charles Square, the Emaus monastery, and at Vyšehrad, until bells all over the city were pealing out the hymn of eternal Prague.

In that instant the sword vanished. Up above, two dark heads appeared over the balustrade of the bridge with its white pillow of snow, as if two black crows had landed there. It was a German patrol, and it peered down with malicious curiosity, wondering why there were so many Czech children down there and what they were up to. But it never found out, because as quick as a flash, the sword had disappeared beneath some child's coat — a winter coat, a sheepskin jacket, or a parka, maybe that boy's, perhaps that girl's. Nobody knew who had it, but it didn't matter. The only thing that could be said for sure was that it was hidden next to a child's heart. For the truth is that the stones of a bridge may be dislodged and overturned, but never a child's heart.

Since then the miraculous sword is in hiding again and no one knows where it is. All we know is that Czech children have taken it into their care, and that it is safe with them and will reappear when the right moment comes.

That's why the legend of the miraculous sword in the Charles Bridge will now have to be told in a different way. It is no longer hidden beneath a stone. No longer will we walk across the bridge and say, "Somewhere here lies our hope and our salvation when things are at their worst." But whenever we meet a Czech child we will say, "This is where it is!" And there it will remain hidden until the time is ripe. Then St. Wenceslas will ride out at the head of the Knights of Blaník to save us. But when he gets to the Charles Bridge, his horse won't stumble against the legendary stone. Instead, a child will run out, pull the sword from under his or her coat, and give it to him. The age-old prophecy will come true, and the Czech lands and all their peoples will enjoy peace and tranquillity for ever and ever.

WRITTEN IN 1940

Translated from the Czech by A. G. Brain

A Psychiatric Mystery

Jaroslav Hašek

I

IT WAS ABOUT TWO O'CLOCK in the morning and Mr. Hurych was walking home from a meeting of teetotalers that evening in a restaurant in Malá Strana. The meeting had lasted so long because they'd been discussing the resignation of the chairman, who'd got mixed up in an ugly affair. He'd been seen drinking a glass of Pilsener beer in a certain establishment. As a man of honor, he had stepped down.

Mr. Hurych, then, was walking home across the Charles Bridge. He walked in the blissful awareness that he was working for the good of mankind. He could still feel the heavy chill of soda water in his stomach, but slightly higher beat a warm, ardent heart that might have easily succumbed to thrombosis had not his doctor forbidden him to drink beer. He had been a teetotaler for half a year now and had thrown himself with determination into the war on alcohol. He was secretary of the Society of Teetotalers, had a paid subscription to *Human Interest*, was learning Esperanto, and ate vegetables.

His thoughts were interrupted by a cry from the river. It was one of those cries in the night so beloved of young poets because it was worth sixteen hellers, that being the amount paid for a line of poetry containing a mysterious cry of unknown origin rising from the river in the quiet of the night.

Mr. Hurych leaned over the balustrade of the bridge and full of dark premonition, called down to the Vltava, "Can I be of any assistance?" He couldn't think of anything better to say at that moment.

While Mr. Hurych was looking inquisitively down at the water, the hairdresser Bílek was walking along the bridge toward Malá Strana. He was not exactly a teetotaler, particularly not that day, but he had no less noble a heart, as imbued with true love for his fellow man as Mr. Hurych's, a golden and dedicated heart.

His sharp eyes discerned that Mr. Hurych was leaning suspiciously over the bridge. Mr. Bílek was a man of action. As silently as a cat and as swiftly as a lynx he crept up on Mr. Hurych from behind, grabbed him by the arms, and tried to pull him to the ground. Mr. Hurych, however, grabbed his unknown assailant by the neck and, with cries of "Police!" both these noble men struggled with each other, while the hairdresser shouted, "Calm down, there's no reason to despair."

A police patrol trotted up and Mr. Bílek, holding Mr. Hurych with all his strength, panted, "Gentlemen, this man tried to jump into the river, and I saved him."

Four experienced hands now seized Mr. Hurych, took him under the arms, and one of the officers began in fatherly tones to dissuade him of his suicidal intentions.

Mr. Hurych was astonished by this situation. "This is all a terrible mistake, gentlemen!" he shouted hysterically. He gave a strange, forced laugh and went on, "You're utterly wrong, gentlemen. I had no intention whatsoever of jumping into the river."

The noble hairdresser, following on behind them, interrupted Mr. Hurych. "I've already saved several people who've tried to jump into the river, but none put up the fight you did. You must be extremely upset. Why, you've torn my vest."

Then the second officer got into the act: "My God, what if everyone tried to kill themselves every time they had a little problem? Everything's going to be just fine again. Whatever has you upset, it'll all be set right. And when you sober up in the morning, you'll see that the world is a pretty nice place after all."

"The world is a beautiful place," said the officer on Mr. Hurych's right. "If people tried to jump in the water every time they took a notion, every second person would drown himself."

Mr. Bílek tugged at Mr. Hurych's coat and added with great emphasis, "Just so you'll know who saved your life, remember, when you sober up, that my name is Bílek and I'm a hairdresser from Smíchov."

Mr. Hurych began to shout hysterically, "Gentlemen, I beg you, let me go! I had no intention of the sort whatsoever. I was merely leaning over the balustrade because I thought I heard someone calling out from below."

"Now look here," said the hairdresser, "are you trying to tell me you didn't want to jump? Gentlemen, I'm an experienced man. The minute I lay eyes on someone, I know whether they intend to jump or not. Sir, if you had not wanted to jump, you would not have struggled so violently. When you think about this tomorrow morning, you'll thank the Lord that your guardian angel sent me to save your life."

Mr. Hurych's patience snapped. He whirled around and flung several very crude insults in the face of that noble and dedicated man.

"This is what a man gets for his kindness," said Mr. Bílek ruefully. "When this gentleman sobers up in the morning, he'll be ashamed to think of how he repaid his rescuer."

Mr. Hurych made an attempt to fling himself on the hairdresser, but stopped when the officers told him they'd have to send for a paddy wagon.

When they were almost at the police station, he tried once more to clarify the situation. "So you don't believe me, then? I swear to you it's all a big misunderstanding."

"Now just you calm down," said the officers soothingly. "Once you've had a good night's sleep and get these silly ideas out of your head, you'll look at life quite differently."

"Oh, my Jesus," groaned Mr. Hurych.

I I

There is a whole series of mental illnesses accompanied by suicide attempts, such as *paralysa progressiva,* paranoia, melancholy, various types of mania, hysteria, and psychosis.

Police physicians are often called in to help attempted suicide victims, and one of their most important psychiatric aids is a system of questions and answers.

The answers victims give help the doctors determine the kind of mental illness involved, since one of the constant symptoms is a confusion in the patient's mind about the meaning of certain ideas and concepts.

And so, a police doctor was called in to evaluate Mr. Hurych's mental state.

Before he arrived, however, the duty officer questioned the altruistic hairdresser and wrote a report.

He, too, could not refrain from trying to ease Mr. Hurych's

gloom by reminding him of the delights of this world. "Everything will be fine again, sir. It'll straighten itself out, even if there's an unhappy love affair behind this. You know what they say: There's lots of good fish in the sea. When you sober up in the morning, sir, you go straight to Mr. Bílek and thank him for saving your life. And if you have family troubles, you can always move out. You mustn't take it so seriously. And if you're in difficult financial straits — and I can't see into your affairs — an honest man can always make a living. Work makes a man more noble."

And what was Mr. Hurych's reply? Covering his face with his hands, he cried out, "In the name of Jesus Christ, I didn't want this to happen!"

Then Mr. Bílek spoke to him again. "I'm the hairdresser, Bílek, from Smíchov, and I want you to feel free to tell me what led you to do it."

Mr. Hurych began to cry.

III

"Bring him in to see me," said the police doctor when he arrived.

They brought Mr. Hurych in. His face wore a terrified look, his lips were white, his hair rumpled.

"Why did you try to jump into the river?"

"I swear I did not try to jump."

"Don't deny it. Mr. Bílek and the officers here all testify that you did. When they attempted to save your life, you fought like a tiger."

"This is awful," groaned Mr. Hurych.

"Tell me, why does the sun set?"

"For God's sake, I beg you, doctor."

"Do you know the names of any free countries in Asia?"

"Please, doctor."

"How much is six times twelve?"

But Mr. Hurych could contain himself no longer, and instead of saying "seventy-two," he gave the police doctor a resounding slap in the face.

Next morning, they took him off to the insane asylum, where he has been under observation for half a year now. So far, the doctors have been unable to determine any awareness on his part that he is mentally ill. According to psychiatry, awareness is one of the signs that recovery is on the way.

Translated from the Czech by Paul Wilson

The Golem

Gustav Meyrink

WE HAD OPENED THE WINDOW to try to get the smell of tobacco out of my little room. The cold night wind now blew in, making the curtain that hung over the door sway to and fro.

"Prokop's worthy headgear would like to take unto itself wings and fly away," said Zwakh, and pointed to the musician's hat, which was flapping its broad brim like black wings.

Joshua Prokop's eyes twinkled.

"It wants to go . . ." he said.

"It wants to go dancing at Loisiček's," Vrieslander finished for him.

Prokop laughed again and, with one hand, started to beat time to the noises borne over the roofs on the wings of the winter breeze. Then, from the wall, he took down my old guitar, and made as though he would pluck its broken strings, while he sang in his cracky falsetto, and with fantastic phrasing, a remarkable song in dialect:

An Bein-del von Ei-sen alt
An Stranz-zen net gar a so kalt
Messinung, a'Raucherl und Rohn
Und immer nurr put-zen . . .

"They sing that old song every evening down at Loisiček's," Zwakh informed me. "Meshuggene old Nephtali Šafránek, with his green shade over his eyes, wheezes it out, accompanied on the accordion by a painted piece of female goods. Really, you, Master Pernath, you ought to go along with us there some evening — perhaps tonight — later, when we're through with the punch, eh? What do you say to it? Isn't your birthday today or something?"

"Yes," urged Prokop, as he closed the window once more, "You come along with us, old fellow-me-lad. It's a thing to see for yourself."

We sat around drinking hot punch, while our thoughts roamed the room.

Vrieslander was carving a puppet.

"Well, Joshua," Zwakh broke the silence, "you've shut us off good and proper from the outer world. Not one word had got itself spoken since you shut the window."

"I was thinking," said Prokop, rather hurriedly, as if apologizing for his own silence, "while the curtain was flapping, how odd it is when the wind plays with inanimate objects. It's almost like a miracle when things that lie about without a particle of life in their bodies suddenly start to flutter. Haven't you ever felt that? Once I stood in a desolate square and watched scraps of paper chasing one another. I couldn't feel the wind, as I was in the shelter of a house, but there they were, all chasing each other, murder in their hearts. Next instant they appeared to have decided on an armistice, but all of a sudden some unendurable puff of bitterness seemed to blow through the lot of them, and off they went again, each hounding on his neighbor till they disappeared round the corner. One solid piece of newspaper only lagged behind; it lay helplessly on the pavement, flapping venomously up and down, like a fish out of water, gasping for air. I couldn't help the thought that rose in me: if we, when all's said and done, aren't similar to these little bits of fluttering paper. Driven hither and thither by some invisible, incomprehensible "wind" that dictates all our actions, while we in our simplicity think we have free will. Supposing life really were nothing but that mysterious whirlwind of which the Bible states, it 'blowest where it listeth, and thou hearest the sound thereof, but canst not tell whence it comest and whither it goeth!' Isn't there a dream in which we fumble in deep pools after silver fish, and catch them, to wake and find nothing in our hands but a cold draught of air blowing through them?"

"Prokop, you're catching that trick of speech from Pernath!" Zwakh regarded the musician suspiciously.

"It's the result of the story of the book, *Ibbur*, we had told to us before you came. Pity you were late and missed it . . . you can see the effect it's had on Prokop." This from Vrieslander.

"Story about a book?"

"Story about a man, rather, who brought the book, and looked very strange. Pernath doesn't know who he is, where he lives, what his name is, or what he wanted. And, for all his visitor's striking appearance, he can't for the life of him describe him."

Zwakh listened attentively.

"Strange," he said, after a pause. "Was the stranger clean-shaven by any chance, and did his eyes slant?"

"I think so," I replied. "That is to say . . . yes . . . yes, I am quite sure of it. Do you know him?"

The puppeteer shook his head. "Only it reminds me of the Golem."

Vrieslander, the artist, laid down his knife.

"The Golem? I've heard of it before. Do you know anything about the Golem, Zwakh?"

"Who can say he knows anything about the Golem?" was Zwakh's rejoinder, as he shrugged his shoulders. "Always they treat it as a legend, till something happens and turns it into actuality again. After which it's talked of for many a day. The rumors wax more and more fantastic, till the whole business gets so exaggerated and overdone that it dies of its own absurdity.

"The original story harks back, so they say, to the sixteenth century. Using long-lost formulas from the cabala, a rabbi is said to have made an artificial man — the so-called Golem — to help ring the bells in the Synagogue and for all kinds of other menial work.

"But he hadn't made a full man, and it was animated by a sort of vegetable half-life. What life it had, too, so the story runs, was only derived from a magic charm placed behind its teeth each day, that drew to itself what was known as the 'free sidereal strength of the universe.'

"One evening, before evening prayers, the rabbi forgot to take the charm out of the Golem's mouth, and it fell into a frenzy. It raged through the dark streets, smashing everything in its path, until the rabbi caught up with it, removed the charm, and destroyed it. Then the Golem collapsed, lifeless. All that was left of it was a small clay image, which you can still see in the Old Synagogue."

"The same rabbi was once summoned to the Imperial Palace by the emperor, where he conjured up the spirits of the dead and made them visible," put in Prokop. "The modern theory is that he used a magic lantern."

"Oh, yes," said Zwakh composedly. "That explanation is foolish enough to appeal to moderns. A magic lantern! As if the Emperor Rudolf, who spent his life chasing after such things, couldn't have spotted a blatant fraud like that at first glance.

"I don't know how the Golem story originated, but this I know: there is something here in this quarter of the town, something that cannot die, and has its being within our midst. From generation to generation, my ancestors have lived in this place, and no one has heard more direct experiences and traditional stories than I have."

Zwakh suddenly ceased speaking. It was obvious his thoughts had gone trailing off into the past.

As he sat there at the table, head on hand, his rosy youthful-looking cheeks contrasting oddly in the lamplight with his snowy hair, I could hardly refrain from comparing his face with the little puppets he had so often shown to me. Curious how the old fellow resembled them! The same expression, and the same cast of countenance.

There are many things on earth that cannot be separated, I pondered. As Zwakh's simple life-history passed before my mind's eye, it struck me as both monstrous and weird that a man such as he, in spite of a better education than that of his forebears (he had, as a matter of fact, been destined for the stage), should suddenly insist on reverting to his dilapidated box of marionettes, trundling once more into the market-place these aged dolls that had acted for the scanty living of his ancestors, and there making them reenact their well-worn histories of clumsy gesture.

I appreciated the reason. He could not endure to be parted from them; their lives were bound up with his, and once he was away from them they changed to thoughts within his brain, where they led him to a restless existence till he returned to them. For that reason did he love them, and trick them out so proudly.

"Won't you tell us some more, Zwakh?" Prokop begged the old man, with a glance at myself and Vrieslander that sought approval.

"I hardly know where to begin," the old man said hesitantly. "Golem stories are all hard telling. Pernath, here, just now was telling us he knew quite well how the stranger looked, but he couldn't describe him. More or less every three and thirty years something takes place in our streets, not so out-of-the-way or startling in itself, yet the terror of it is too strong for either explanation or excuse.

"Always it happens that an apparition makes its appearance — an utterly strange man, clean-shaven, of yellow complexion, Mongolian type, in antiquated clothes of a bygone day; it comes from the direction of Alteschulgasse, stalks through the Ghetto with a queer groping, stumbling kind of gait, as if afraid of falling over, and quite suddenly — is gone.

"Usually it is seen to disappear round a corner. At other times it is said to have described a circle and gone back to the point whence it started — an old house, close by the synagogue.

"Some people will tell how they have seen it coming toward them down a street, but, as they walked boldly to meet it, it would grow smaller and smaller, like an ordinary figure will do as it moves away from you, and finally it disappears completely.

"Sixty-six years ago there must have been a particularly lively scare of this sort, for I remember — I was a tiny youngster at the time — that the house on Alteschulgasse was searched from top to bottom. It is also said that there is a room with a barred window, but no entrance. They hung washing out of every window, and the room was discovered. As the only means of reaching it, a man let himself down a rope from the roof, to see in. But no sooner did he get near the window than the rope broke and the poor fellow fractured his skull upon the pavement. And when they wanted, later on, to try again, opinions differed so about the situation of the window that they gave it up.

"I myself encountered the Golem for the first time in my life nearly three and thirty years ago. I met it in a little alley, and we ran right into one another. I still cannot remember now very distinctly what went on in my mind at that encounter. Heaven forbid anyone should spend his life in perpetual expectation, day in, day out, of meeting the Golem. At that moment, before I had seen anything, something cried out in me, loud and shrill: 'The Golem!' At that instant someone stumbled out of a doorway and the strange figure passed me by. Next moment I was surrounded by a sea of white, frightened faces, everyone asking if I had seen it.

"As I replied, I was aware for the first time that my tongue had been released from a clamp. I was quite surprised to find I could move my limbs, for I realized now, for the space of a heartbeat, I must have endured a sort of paralytic shock from surprise.

"I have given the subject much thought, and the nearest I can get to the truth of it seems to be this: that once in every generation a spiritual disturbance zigzags, like a flash of lightning, right through the Ghetto, taking possession of the souls of the living to some end we know not of, and rising in the form of a wraith that appears to our senses in the guise of a human entity that once, centuries ago, maybe, lived here, and is craving materialization.

"Maybe, too, it lurks within our midst, day after day, and we know it not. Neither do our ears register the sound of the tuning fork till it is brought in contact with the wood, which it forces into sympathetic vibration.

"Think of the crystal, resolving itself, it knows not how but in accordance with its own immutable laws, from the formless, to a definite, ordered shape. May it not be even so in the world of the spirit? Who shall say? Just as in thundery weather the electric tension in the atmosphere will increase to a point past endurance, and eventually give birth to lightning, may it not be that the whole mass of stagnant thought infecting the air of the Ghetto needs clearing from time to time by some kind of mysterious explosion, something potent in its workings. Something forces the dreams of the subconscious up into the light of day — like a lightning stroke — giving rise to an object that, could we but read its riddle, symbolizes, both in ways and appearance, the mass soul.

"And, just as Nature has her own happenings that foreshadow the advent of the lightning, so do certain forbidding signs portend the arrival of this phantom within our world of fact. The plaster peeling from an old wall will adopt the shape of a running human form; and stony faces stare from the ice flowers formed by the frost upon the windowpanes. Sand from the rooftops falls in a different way from usual, filling the apprehensive passerby with the impression it had been thrown by some invisible spirit, trying to form, from the hiding place wherein it lurks, all kinds of unfamiliar outlines. No matter what the object one beholds — be it wickerwork, all one color, or the uneven surface of human skin — we are still obsessed with this disconcerting gift of finding everywhere these ominous, significant shapes, that assume in our dreams the proportions of giants. And always, through these ghostly strivings of these troops of thoughts, endeavoring to gnaw their way through the wall of actuality, runs, like a scarlet thread, a torturing certitude that our own mental consciousness, strive as we may, is being sucked dry, deliberately, that the phantom may attain to concrete form. . . ."

"Now for the head" — all at once, in Vrieslander's cheery tones. And he took a small billet of wood from his pocket and started to carve.

I pushed my armchair into the background, out of the light. My eyes were heavy with weariness.

The hot water for the punch was sizzling in the kettle and Joshua started to fill our glasses round again. Softly, very softly, the sound of dance music stole through the closed window, fitfully, now coming, now going, according to the caprices of the wind.

Wouldn't I clink glasses with him? the musician wanted to know, after a pause.

But I made no answer. So loath was I to make any kind of movement, I would not even open my mouth. I might have almost been asleep, such was the feeling of utter quiet that now possessed my soul. I had to glance now and again at the twinkling blade of Vrieslander's pocketknife as he cut small chips of the wood, to assure myself that I was really awake.

From afar I heard Zwakh's rumbling voice as he told wonderful stories about puppets and narrated the plots of his plays.

Vrieslander was still hacking away at his puppet head; you could hear the scraping of his knife upon the wood.

The sound of it somehow distressed me, and I looked up to see if it would not soon be finished.

The head, turning about as it did in the carver's hand, looked alive. It seemed to be peering into all the corners of the room. At last its eyes rested upon me. It appeared pleased to have found me at last.

And I, in my turn, was unable to turn my eyes away. Stonily I stared at that little wooden face.

The carver's knife seemed to hesitate a little, then suddenly made a strong, decisive cut, informing the wooden head, all at once, with terrifying personality. I recognized the yellow countenance of the stranger who had brought me the book.

There my powers of discernment ended. It had lasted only one moment, but I could feel my heart cease to beat, and then bound forward agonizingly.

The face, none the less, remained in my mind. Just as it had done before.

It was I myself . . . I and none other . . . and I lay there on Vrieslander's lap, gaping.

My eyes were wandering around the room, and strange fingers laid their touch upon my head.

All of a sudden I was aware of Zwakh's face distorted with excitement. I could hear his voice: "God! It's the Golem!"

A short struggle had ensued, while they had tried to wrest Vrieslander's work from his hand. But he fended them off, and crying with a laugh, "All right! I've made a mess of this job," had opened the window and flung the head into the street below.

Consciousness left me, and I dove into deep darkness veined with shimmering golden threads, and when I awoke again, as it seemed, after a long, long time, I heard the wooden head strike the pavement outside.

Translated from the German by Madge Pemberton

The Legend of the Old Town Clock

Alois Jirásek

HORDES OF PEOPLE flocked to the City Hall in the Old Town, and yet there was neither a town meeting being held, nor an important trial, but still they kept coming. They all stood around waiting expectantly, for an hour or more, in crowded discomfort. They were there to gaze at the tower with its wonder of wonders, the new clock. Everybody was talking about it — in all the quarters of the city, inside noble palaces, in poor people's houses, in taverns and shops, and on the streets: this new clock in the City Hall tower in the Old Town was not like other clocks, but was so marvelous that there was no other like it in the whole world. Townsfolk, craftsmen, idlers, students, women, the young and old, all were standing on tiptoe, craning their necks, their eyes glued to the big dial, which showed twenty-four hours, and was crisscrossed with lines and golden circles. Beneath it was a board with painted pictures of the twelve signs of the zodiac. To the right were stone statues, a skeleton symbolizing death, and a Turk holding a sack of coins. The air was filled with the sounds of many voices like the babble of running water.

The noise would always suddenly die away when a bell began to toll from the new clock. Amid cries of amazement, many hands would point in astonishment at the figure of Death, which was pulling a rope that rang the bell. Then two small windows over the clock face opened, and the figures of two apostles appeared in them and moved on, making way for the others, till all twelve apostles had appeared in the windows. Each turned momentarily to face the audience before resuming his advance from west to east. Finally the figure of Jesus could be seen, hands raised in benediction. Some doffed their hats, others crossed themselves, others kept watching the figure of Death, grinning at Judas and at the figure of the Turk next to it, the latter shaking his head, refusing to let Death take him just yet. Then above the windows, a stone cock would crow, the clock would strike the hour, and the figures were all motionless again for another hour. And again the voices started the relentless hum of conversation. They spoke of the clock's originator, endowed with special gifts and talents; all admired Master Hanuš, who had built it.

Even learned men from the university, masters and doctors in their academic robes, standing together as they examined the clock, had praise for its builder. They spoke in Latin, solemnly, with grave faces. But they discussed only the circles and lines and signs on the dial. They smiled tolerantly at the figures of the apostles and Death and the others. One old sage remarked scornfully to his students that a bell-pulling skeleton and a crowing rooster and tricks like that served only to entertain the populace. Then he pointed out to them that this clock was valuable to all scholars and especially to astronomers, because it showed how the sun revolved around the earth, it showed the signs of the zodiac, and under what sign we were at any given time, when the sun would rise and set on any particular day, where in the horizon the sun stood at any particular time, farther in winter, closer in summer. The clock, he said, did not need any foolish embellishments.

The learned masters grew silent as a group of councilmen

and Old Town officials, all in ceremonial garb, made their way through the ornate portal, heading for the clock tower. The crowd parted to make way for them, and all eyes turned on them, especially on one pale-faced, dark-haired elderly man. He was clad in the dark robes of a master of his craft, and walked right next to the governor. The word got around that this was Master Hanuš, the maker of the clock. People crowded around, craning their necks to get a glimpse of him.

Everybody, even the people from the university, greeted him respectfully. He responded with courtesy, and as soon as the city fathers stopped under the clock, he at once proceeded to explain its workings. He spoke of the sun and the stars, he pointed out how the clock showed the position of the moon at any given time, whether waxing or waning. He told them about the twelve zodiac signs, of which six were over the earth and six under it. In addition, he said, the clock marked the days of the week, the month, and the seasons, including all the holidays for the year. The people listened in respectful silence, and even the professors paid heed, looking owlish, and sagely nodded their heads in agreement.

When Master Hanuš finished, the crowd cheered, but he modestly turned to the councilmen and invited them to accompany him to the tower, so that he might explain to them the workings of the clock's machinery, the precision of all the weights, cogs, and wheels, especially as the clock was about to strike. Inside the tower, the guests marveled at the complex, artful machinery, each cog with its prescribed task. How could a single human brain have invented it all? They grew more and more amazed, as Master Hanuš showed and explained to them the four parts of the clock, each with its weights and counterweights. They especially admired the fourth section, where a large wheel had 365 cogs, one for each day of the year. It would take a whole year, the master told them, for that wheel to make one revolution.

The clock machinery worked accurately, as though it had a mind and a soul of its own, and only he understood all its workings. One of the council, Jan, also a clock maker, admitted candidly that he could not understand it at all, that this clock was doubtlessly divinely inspired. He himself was an old master of his craft, he said, but he would surely lose his mind if he had to care for or repair this clock.

One of the professors of Charles University who had come along told the assembled company that he had traveled far and wide, and had visited Italy and France, where he had seen some fine big clocks, but never had he seen the like of this one. "I do not believe that a more magnificent one could be found anywhere else in the whole world," he said, "unless Master Hanuš himself should build it."

The governor gave a start and glanced at his councillors, who quickly returned his look. All had simultaneously been struck by the same thought: that such a thing might happen. They turned to Hanuš, who smiled, and said disarmingly that he was happy to have been able to complete this complex clock, and that he thanked God for having done so. But the governor left the clock tower less happily than he had entered it. A worrisome thought had been planted in his mind, as well as in the minds of the elders: namely, that Master Hanuš might make another such clock elsewhere, that other places would then have such a marvel of their own.

The fame of the Prague clock spread over the crown lands of Bohemia and into foreign countries. Every visitor who came to town went to see it, and then talked about it after he returned home. Messengers came from various towns, at home and abroad, to ask Master Hanuš to build a similar clock for them. The governor and his council grew uneasy. They did not wish to share their glory with anyone; they wanted their clock to remain the only one of its kind. They sat in secret session to consider what should be done to this end. They agreed that Hanuš might be tempted by foreign promises of a reward. Perhaps he was already at work on a new clock, they thought, a clock that would be even better, since he spent so much time in his workshop, working on something or other. In order to make sure that nobody would compete with them, they decided to commit a terrible deed.

Master Hanuš was seated in his workshop behind a large table, and was busy drawing plans for some complex machinery on a large sheet of paper, by the light of two candles. The shutters were drawn, and there was a fire burning in the fireplace. It was night. The street outside was dark and deserted. The house, too, was quiet. The clock maker was so absorbed in his task that he did not hear footsteps on the stairs outside. He did not even turn around when the door opened and three men came in, wearing cloaks and hoods that covered much of their faces. Only after they had come up to him did he stop his work to look at them. But before he had time to ask what they wanted, two of them seized him while the third blew out the candles. Then they gagged him and pulled him to the glowing fireplace.

These men had let themselves in with a pass key, and nobody in the household knew of their presence or heard their muffled footsteps, either as they entered or as they left the house. They had come like shadows, and like shadows they disappeared into the night. It was not until the following morning that their crime was discovered. The apprentices found Master Hanuš, still gagged, racked with fever, and with a bandage over his eyes. Then Hanuš told his horrified household and neighbors what had happened. The intruders had put his eyes out and placed the bandage around his head. He could not remember much more, as he had passed out.

News of the crime inflamed the whole city. Public feeling ran high, but no trace of the criminals could be found. People whispered various rumors and repeated what Hanuš himself had said after he had recovered slightly: "Stop looking for the culprits, they will not be found even though they are nearby."

He would say no more, but people suspected that he could have spoken had he wished to do so. But he remained silent. He sat, sad and motionless, in the corner of his old workshop, like some caged bird on his perch. All his tools and implements hung idle, and dust gathered on his books and charts. For him, all was in total darkness, he could no longer touch his work. Without it, he grew restive. What also troubled him was the ingratitude that he had reaped for his accomplishment. In his mind he kept hearing the words of one of the criminals on that fateful night: "Well, now you won't build any more such clocks!"

This, he felt, was his reward. He fretted more and more and his body grew weaker and weaker. Finally, he felt that his end was near. Mustering his last bit of strength, he had one of his former apprentices lead him to the city hall in the Old Town. As usual, a crowd had gathered by the tower, waiting for the clock to strike. But nobody recognized him, he had aged so much. He was thinner, his cheeks sunken, his hair gray, his skin the color of parchment. At the door he met several of the councillors, but they avoided him. Nobody greeted him. None of them had been pleased when he had sent word he was coming, that he had had a new idea about how to improve the clock so the weights would move more smoothly.

He had his guide take him to the fourth part of the clock-works, the most complex of all. In his darkness he could only hear the clicking and ticking of the many parts. As he stood there, listening, he thought of the council, of how blindness had been his reward, of how the council had made him suffer, only to be able to boast before the whole world of his great achievement.

Just then, the bell started to toll, the figure of Death outside pulling the rope. The fleeting hour was announced. Death called. The windows opened, the apostles started revolving. Master Hanuš trembled. He held out his right hand over the clockwork, and then, as though he could see clearly, his bony fingers began manipulating the machinery. When he drew back his hand, the wheels started revolving madly, ticking and squeaking, roaring and ticking. Then they ground to a standstill. The figures froze where they stood. The apostles did not complete their hourly journey. The cock did not crow. Outside, the excited throng screamed. The councilmen ran to the tower. But the clockworks stood motionless, and their builder lay on the floor beside them in a dead faint. He was carried home and died soon afterward.

The clock continued to stand still, as there was no one to repair it. Only much later was it somewhat restored and is working to this day, a matchless curiosity.

Translated from the Czech by Marie K. Holeček

Description of a Struggle

Franz Kafka

AT ABOUT MIDNIGHT a few people rose, bowed, shook hands, said it had been a pleasant evening, and then passed through the wide doorway into the vestibule to put on their coats. The hostess stood in the middle of the room and made graceful bowing movements, causing the dainty folds in her skirt to move up and down.

I sat at a tiny table — it had three curved, thin legs — sipping my third glass of benedictine, and while I drank I surveyed my little store of pastry, which I myself had picked out and arranged in a pile.

Then I saw my new acquaintance, somewhat disheveled and out of shape, appear at the doorpost of an adjoining room; but I tried to look away for it was no concern of mine. He, however, came toward me and, smiling absentmindedly at my occupation, said, "Excuse me for disturbing you, but until this very moment, I've been sitting alone with my girl in the room next door. Ever since half past ten. Lord, what an evening! I know it isn't right for me to be telling you this, for we hardly know one another. We only met on the stairs this evening and exchanged a few words as guests of the same house. And now — but you must forgive me, please — my happiness just cannot be contained, I can't help it. And since I have no other acquaintance here whom I can trust — "

I looked at him sadly — the piece of fruitcake which I had in my mouth did not taste particularly good — and said into his rather flushed face: "I'm glad of course that you consider me trustworthy, but displeased that you have confided in me. And you yourself, if you weren't in such a state, would know how improper it is to talk about an amorous girl to a man sitting alone drinking schnapps."

When I said this, he sat down with a jolt, leaned back in his chair, and let his arms hang down. Then he pressed them back, his elbows pointed, and began talking in rather a loud voice, "Only a little while ago we were alone in that room, Annie and I. And I kissed her, I kissed her — her mouth, her ears, her shoulders. Oh, my Lord and Savior!"

A few guests, suspecting ours to be a rather more animated conversation, approached us closer, yawning. Whereupon I stood up and said, so that all could hear, "All right then, if you insist, I'll go with you, but I repeat: it's ridiculous to climb up the Laurenziberg now, in winter and in the middle of the night. Besides, it's freezing, and as it has been snowing, the roads out there are like skating rinks. Well, as you like — "

At first he gazed at me in astonishment and parted his wet lips; but then, noticing the guests who had approached quite close, he laughed, stood up, and said, "I think the cold will do us good; our clothes are full of heat and smoke; what's more, I'm slightly tipsy without having drunk very much; yes, let's say good-bye and go."

So we went to the hostess, and as he kissed her hand, she said, "I'm glad to see you looking so happy today."

Touched by the kindness of these words, he kissed her hand again; whereupon she smiled. I had to drag him away. In the vestibule stood a housemaid, whom we hadn't seen before. She helped us into our coats and then took a small lantern to light us down the stairs. Her neck was bare save for a black velvet ribbon around her throat; her loosely clothed body was stooped and kept stretching as she went down the stairs before us, holding the lantern low. Her cheeks were flushed, for she had drunk some wine, and in the weak lamplight which filled the whole stairwell, I could see her lips trembling.

At the foot of the stairs she put down the lantern, took a step toward my acquaintance, embraced him, kissed him, and remained in the embrace. Only when I pressed a coin into her hand did she drowsily detach her arms from him, slowly open the front door, and let us out into the night.

Over the deserted, evenly lit street stood a large moon in a slightly clouded, and therefore unusually extended, sky. On the frozen snow one had to take short steps.

Hardly were we outside when I evidently began to feel very gay. I raised my legs, let my joints crack, I shouted a name down the street as though a friend of mine had just vanished around the corner; leaping, I threw my hat in the air and caught it boastfully.

My acquaintance, however, walked on beside me, unconcerned. He held his head bent. He didn't even speak.

This surprised me, for I had calculated that once I had got him away from the party, he would give vent to his joy. Now I too could calm down. No sooner had I given him an encouraging slap on the back than I suddenly no longer understood his mood, and withdrew my hand. Since I had no use for it, I stuck it in the pocket of my coat.

So we walked on in silence. Listening to the sound of our steps, I couldn't understand why I was incapable of keeping step with my acquaintance — especially since the air was clear and I could see his legs quite plainly. Here and there someone leaned out of a window and watched us.

On turning into Ferdinand Boulevard I realized that my

acquaintance had begun to hum a melody from the *Dollar Princess*. It was low, but I could hear it distinctly. What did this mean? Was he trying to insult me? As for me, I was ready to do without not only this music, but the walk as well. Why wasn't he speaking to me, anyway? And if he didn't need me, why hadn't he left me in peace in the warm room with the benedictine and the pastry? It certainly wasn't I who had insisted on this walk. Besides, I could have gone for a walk on my own. I had merely been at a party, had saved an ungrateful young man from disgrace, and was now wandering about in the moonlight. That was all right, too. All day in the office, evenings at a party, at night in the streets, and nothing to excess. A way of life so natural that it borders on the excessive!

Yet my acquaintance was still behind me. Indeed, he even quickened his steps when he realized that he had fallen in the rear. No word was uttered, nor could it be said that we were running. But I wondered if it wouldn't be a good idea to turn down a side street; after all, I wasn't obliged to go on this walk with him. I could go home alone and no one could stop me. Then, secretly, I could watch my acquaintance pass the entrance to my street. Good-bye dear acquaintance! On reaching my room I'll feel warm, I'll light the lamp in its iron stand on my table, and when I've done that I'll lie back in my armchair which stands on the torn oriental carpet. Pleasant prospects! Why not? But then? The lamp will shine in the warm room, shine on my chest as I lie in the armchair. Then I'll cool off and spend hours alone between the painted walls and the floor which, reflected in the gilt-framed mirror hanging on the rear wall, appears slanted.

My legs were growing tired and I had already decided to go home and lie down, when I began to wonder if, before going away, I ought to say good-night to my acquaintance. But I was too timid to go away without a word and too weak to call to him out loud. So I stood still, leaned against the moonlit wall of a house, and waited.

My acquaintance came sailing down the pavement toward me as fast as though he expected me to catch him. He winked at me, suggesting some agreement which I had apparently forgotten.

"What's up?" I asked.

"Oh, nothing," he said. "I only wanted to ask your opinion about that housemaid who kissed me on the staircase. Who is the girl? Have you ever seen her before? No? Nor have I. Was she a housemaid at all? I had meant to ask you this before, while she was walking down the stair in front of us."

"I saw at once by her red hands that she's a housemaid, and not even the first housemaid, and when I gave her the money I felt her hard skin."

"But that merely proves that she has been some time in service, which no doubt is the case."

"You may be right about that. In that light one couldn't distinguish everything, but her face reminded me of the elder daughter of an officer I happen to know."

"Not me," he said.

"That won't stop me going home; it's late and I have to be in the office early. One sleeps badly there." Whereupon I put out my hand to say good-bye to him.

"Whew, what a cold hand!" he cried. "I wouldn't like to go home with a hand like that. You should let yourself be kissed, too, my friend. That was an omission. Still, you can make up for it. But sleep? On a night like this? What an idea! Just think how many thoughts a blanket smothers while one lies alone in bed, and how many unhappy dreams it keeps warm."

"I neither smother anything nor warm anything," I said.

"Oh, go on!" He concluded, "You're a humorist!"

He began walking again and I followed without realizing it, for I was busy thinking of what he had said.

From these words I imagined that my acquaintance suspected in me something which, although it wasn't there, made me nevertheless rise in his estimation by his suspecting it. So it was just as well I hadn't gone home. Who knows, this man — thinking of housemaid affairs while walking beside me, his mouth steaming with cold — might be capable of bestowing on me in the eyes of the world a value without my having to work for it. Let's pray the girls won't spoil him! By all means let them kiss and hug him, that's their duty and his right, but they mustn't carry him off. After all, when they kiss him they also kiss me a little — with the corners of their mouths, so to speak. But if they carry him off, then they steal him from me. And he must always remain with me, always. Who is to protect him, if not I? And he's so stupid. Someone says to him in February: Come up the Laurenziberg — and off he goes. And supposing he falls down now, or catches cold? Suppose some jealous man appears from the Postgasse and attacks him? What will happen to me? Am I to be just kicked out of the world? I'll believe that when I see it! No, he won't get rid of me.

Tomorrow he'll be talking to Fraulein Anna, about ordinary things at first, as is natural, but suddenly he won't be able to keep it from her any longer: Last night, Annie, after the party, you remember, I was with a man the like of whom you've certainly never seen. He looked — how can I describe him to you? — like a stick dangling in the air with a black-haired skull on top. His body was clad in a lot of small, dull-yellow patches of cloth which covered him completely because they hung closely about him in the still air of last night. Well, Annie, does that spoil your appetite? It does? In that case it's my fault, then. I told the whole thing badly. If only you'd seen him, walking timidly beside me, reading infatuation on my face (which wasn't very difficult), and going a long way ahead of me so as not to disturb me. I think, Annie, you'd have laughed a bit and been a bit afraid; but I was glad of his company. For where were you, Annie? You were in your bed, and your bed was far away — it might just as well have been in Africa. But sometimes I really felt as though the starry sky rose and fell with the gasping of his flat chest. You think I'm exaggerating? No, Annie. Upon my soul, no. Upon my soul, which belongs to you, no.

And I didn't spare my acquaintance — we had just reached the first steps of the Franzenquai — the smallest fraction of the humiliation he must have felt at making such a speech. Save that my thoughts grew blurred at this moment, for the Moldau and the quarter of the town on the farther shore lay together in the dark. A number of lights burning there teased the eye.

We crossed the road in order to reach the railing along the river, and there we stood still. I found a tree to lean against. Because of the cold blowing up from the water, I put on my gloves, sighed for no good reason, as one is inclined to do at night beside a river, but then I wanted to walk on. My acquaintance, however, was staring into the water, and didn't budge. Then he moved closer to the railing; his legs were already against the iron bar, he propped his elbows up and laid his forehead in his hand. What next? After all, I was shivering and had to put up the collar of my coat. My acquaintance stretched himself — his back, shoulders, neck — and held the upper half of his body, which rested on his taut arms, bent over the railing.

"Oh well, memories," said I. "Yes, even remembering in itself is sad, yet how much more its object! Don't let yourself in for things like that, it's not for you and not for me. It only weakens one's present position without strengthening the former one — nothing is more obvious — quite apart from the fact that the former one doesn't need strengthening. Do you think I have no memories? Oh, ten for every one of yours. Now, for instance, I could remember sitting on a bench in L. It was in the evening, also near a river. In summer, of course. And on such evenings it's my habit to pull up my legs and put my arms around them. I had leaned my head against the wooden back of the bench, and from there I watched the cloudlike mountains on the other shore. A violin was playing softly in the hotel by the river. Now and again on both shores trains chuffed by amid shining smoke."

Turning suddenly around, my acquaintance interrupted me; he almost looked as though he were surprised to see me still here. "Oh, I could tell you much more," I said, nothing else.

"Just imagine," he began, "and it always happens like this. Today, as I was going downstairs to take a short walk before the evening party, I couldn't help being surprised by the way my hands dangled about in my cuffs, and they were doing it so gaily. Which promptly made me think: Just wait, something's going to happen today. And it did, too." He said this while turning to go and looked at me, his eyes wide and smiling.

So I had already got as far as that. He could tell me things like that and at the same time smile and look at me with big eyes. And I — I had to restrain myself from putting my arm around his shoulders and kissing him on the eyes as a reward for having absolutely no use for me. But the worst was that even that could no longer do any harm because it couldn't change anything, for now I had to go away, away at any price.

While I was still trying urgently to think of some means by which I could stay at least a little while longer with my acquaintance, it occurred to me that perhaps my long body displeased him by making him feel too small. And this thought — although it was late at night and we had hardly met a soul — tormented me so much that while walking I bent my back until my hands reached my knees. But in order to prevent my acquaintance from noticing my intentions I changed my position only very gradually, tried to divert his attention from myself, once even turning him toward the river, pointing out to him the trees on the Schutzeninsel and the way the bridge lamps were reflected in the river.

But wheeling suddenly around, he looked at me — I hadn't quite finished yet — and said, "What's this? You're all crooked! What on earth are you up to?"

"Quite right. You're very observant," said I, my head on the seam of his trousers, which was why I couldn't look up properly.

"Enough of that! Stand up straight! What nonsense!"

"No," I said, my face close to the ground, "I'll stay as I am."

"You really can annoy a person, I must say. Such a waste of time! Come on, stop it."

"The way you shout! In the quiet of the night!" I said.

"Oh well, just as you like," he added, and after a while, "It's a quarter to one." He had evidently seen the time on the clock of the Muhlenturm.

I promptly stood up straight as though I'd been pulled up

by the hair. For a while I kept my mouth open, to let my agitation escape. I understood: he was dismissing me. There was no place for me near him, or if there were one, at least it could not be found. Why, by the way, was I so intent on staying with him? No, I ought to go away — and this at once — to my relatives and friends who were waiting for me. But if I didn't have any relatives and friends then I must fend for myself (what was the good of complaining!), but I must leave here no less quickly. For in his eyes nothing could redeem me any longer, neither my height, my appetite, nor my cold hand. But if I were of the opinion that I had to remain with him, it was a dangerous opinion.

"I didn't need your information," I said, which happened to be true.

"Thank God you're standing up straight again. All I said was that it's a quarter to one."

"That's all right," said I, and stuck two fingernails in the gaps between my chattering teeth. "If I didn't need your information, how much less do I need an explanation. The fact is, I need nothing but your mercy. Please take back what you said just now!"

"That it's a quarter to one? But with pleasure, especially since a quarter to one passed long ago."

He lifted his right arm, flicked his hand, and listened to the castanet-like sound of his cuff links.

Obviously, this is the time for the murder. I'll stay with him and slowly he'll draw the dagger — the handle of which he is already holding in his pocket — along his coat, and then plunge it into me. It's unlikely that he'll be surprised at the simplicity of it all — yet maybe he will, who knows? I won't scream, I'll just stare at him as long as my eyes can stand it.

"Well?" he said.

In the front of a distant coffeehouse with black window-panes a policeman let himself glide over the pavement like a skater. His sword hampering him, he took it in his hand, and now he glided along for quite a while, finally ending up almost describing a circle. At last he yodeled weakly and, melodies in his head, began once more to skate.

It wasn't until the arrival of this policeman — who, two hundred feet from an imminent murder, saw and heard only himself — that I began to feel a certain fear. I realized that whether I allowed myself to be stabbed or ran away, my end had come. Would it not be better, then, to run away and thus expose myself to a difficult and therefore more painful death? I could not immediately put my finger on the reasons in favor of this form of death, but I couldn't afford to spend my last remaining seconds looking for reasons. There would be time for that later provided I had the determination, and the determination I had.

I had to run away, it would be quite easy. At the turning to the left onto the Charles Bridge I could jump to the right into the Karlsgasse. It was winding, there were dark doorways, and taverns still open; I didn't need to despair.

As we stepped from under the arch at the end of the quay onto the Kreuzherrenplatz, I ran into that street with my arms raised. But in front of a small door in the Seminarkirche I fell, for there was a step I had not expected. It made a little noise, and the next street lamp was sufficiently far away, so I lay in the dark.

From a tavern opposite came a fat woman with a lantern to see what had happened in the street. The piano within continued playing, but fainter, with only one hand, because the pianist had turned toward the door which, until now ajar, had been opened wide by a man in a high-buttoned coat. He spat and then hugged the woman so hard she was obliged to raise the lantern in order to protect it.

"Nothing's happened!" he shouted into the room, whereupon they both turned, went inside, and the door was closed.

When I tried to get up, I fell down again. "Sheer ice," I said, and felt a pain in my knee. Yet I was glad that the people in the tavern hadn't seen me and that I could go on lying here peacefully until dawn.

My acquaintance had apparently walked on as far as the bridge without having noticed my absence, for it was some time before he joined me. I saw no signs of surprise as he bent down over me — lowering little more than his neck, exactly like a hyena — and stroked me with a soft hand. He passed it up and down my cheekbone and then laid his palm on my forehead. "You've hurt yourself, eh? Well, it's icy and one must be careful — didn't you tell me so yourself? Does your head ache? No? Oh, the knee. Hm. That's bad."

But it didn't occur to him to help me up. I supported my head with my right hand, my elbow on a cobblestone, and said, "Here we are together again." And as my fear was beginning to return, I pressed both hands against his shinbone in order to push him away. "Do go away," I said.

He had his hands in his pockets and looked up the empty street, then at the Seminarkirche, then up at the sky. At last, at the sound of a carriage in one of the nearby streets, he remembered me: "Why don't you say something, my friend? Do you feel sick? Why don't you get up? Shall I look for a cab? If you like, I'll get you some wine from the tavern. In any case, you mustn't lie here in the cold. Besides, we wanted to go up the Laurenziberg."

"Of course," I said, and got up on my own, but with great

pain. I began to sway, and had to look severely at the statue of Charles IV to be sure of my position. However, even this would not have helped me had I not remembered that I was loved by a girl with a black velvet ribbon around her neck, if not passionately, at least faithfully. And it really was kind of the moon to shine on me, too, and out of modesty I was about to place myself under the arch of the tower bridge when it occurred to me that the moon, of course, shone on everything. So I happily spread out my arms in order fully to enjoy the moon. And by making swimming movements with my weary arms it was easy for me to advance without pain or difficulty. To think that I had never tried this before! My head lay in the cool air and it was my right knee that flew best; I praised it by patting it. And I remembered that once upon a time I didn't altogether like my acquaintance, who was probably still walking below me, and the only thing that pleased me about the whole business was that my memory was good enough to remember even a thing like that. But I couldn't afford to do much thinking, for I had to go on swimming to prevent myself from sinking too low. However, to avoid being told later that anyone could swim on the pavement and that it wasn't worth mentioning, I raised myself above the railing by increasing my speed and swam in circles around the statue of every saint I encountered. At the fifth — I was holding myself just above the footpath by imperceptible flappings — my acquaintance gripped my hand. There I stood once more on the pavement and felt a pain in my knee.

"I've always admired," said my acquaintance, clutching me with one hand and pointing with the other at the statue of St. Ludmila, "I've always admired the hands of this angel here to the left. Just see how delicate they are! Real angel's hands!

Have you ever seen anything like them? You haven't, but I have, for this evening I kissed hands — "

But for me there was now a third possibility of perishing. I didn't have to let myself be stabbed, I didn't have to run away, I could simply throw myself into the air. Let him go up his Laurenziberg, I won't interfere with him, not even by running away will I interfere with him.

And now I shouted, "Out with your stories! I no longer want to hear scraps. Tell me everything from beginning to end. I won't listen to less, I warn you. But I'm burning to hear the whole thing." When he looked at me I stopped shouting. "And you can count on my discretion! Tell me everything that's on your mind. You've never had so discreet a listener as I."

And rather low, close to his ear, I said, "And you don't need to be afraid of me, that's quite unnecessary."

I heard him laugh.

"Yes, yes," I said. "I believe that. I don't doubt it." And so saying I pinched him in the calves — where they were exposed. But he didn't feel it. Whereupon I said to myself, "Why walk with this man? You don't love him, nor do you hate him, because all he cares about is a girl and it's not even certain that she wears a white dress. So to you this man is indifferent — I repeat: indifferent. But he is also harmless, that too has been proven. So walk on with him up the Laurenziberg, for you are already on your way. It's a beautiful night, but let him do the talking and enjoy yourself after your fashion, for this is the very best way (say it in a whisper) to protect yourself."

Translated from the German by Tania and James Stern

G M

Gustav Meyrink

"MACKINTOSH, THAT MORON, is back again."

The news spread through town like sparks through a field of stubble.

Everyone, but everyone, remembered George Mackintosh, the German-American who had walked out on Prague just five years ago. They couldn't forget his stunts any more than they could forget that dark, chiseled face of his that had now resurfaced on Příkopy Street.

What could he want here this time?

They had ousted him slowly but surely. Everyone had been in on it, one under a veil of friendship, another through treachery and false rumors, with a pinch of prudent slander from all — and eventually, all those little rascalities added up to such a foul heap of filth that it probably would have crushed anyone else, but all it did to the American was nudge him out of town.

Mackintosh had a face as sharp as a penknife and exceedingly long legs. Even for those who give no credence to racial theories it was hard to take.

They despised him thoroughly; and for his part, instead of trying to placate them and making an effort to adapt to the local ways of thinking, Mackintosh always stood apart. He was constantly coming up with something novel: hypnosis, spiritualism, palm reading, once even a symbolic interpretation of *Hamlet*.

This, of course, brought the otherwise jovial burghers to a boil, especially budding geniuses like Mr. Tewinger of the *Tagblatt*, who was on the verge of publishing his very own book titled *Shakespeare, as I Understand Him*.

So that "thorn in the side" is back again and living with his servants from India at the Red Sun Hotel.

"It's definitely only a temporary thing, then?" inquired one of Mackintosh's old acquaintances.

"Yes, of course, until I can move into my own home on the fifteenth of August. I've purchased a house on Ferdinand Boulevard, you see."

The city's jaw dropped several inches: a house on Ferdinand Boulevard! Where did the old swindler come up with the money? And Indian servants to boot. Well, we'll see how long he lasts!

Naturally Mackintosh had another novelty: an electric-powered device said to be capable of sniffing out gold veins in the earth — a modern-day divining rod of sorts.

Most people were skeptical: "If it were of any worth at all, someone else would have discovered it already!"

But there was no denying the American had become extremely rich in the five years since he had left the city. At least that was what the investigation of the Schniffer and Edam Information Bureau had confirmed.

And indeed, not even a week had passed before Mackintosh bought himself yet another building. His holdings criss-crossed the city with no apparent plan: one at the fruit market, another on Panská Street. But every one of them was in the city center.

For God's sake, could he be making a run for mayor?

No one could make heads or tails out of it.

"Have you seen his calling card yet? Just look at it! If it isn't the most impudent thing I've ever seen — nothing but a monogram — no name at all! Says he doesn't need a name anymore with all the money he's got!"

Mackintosh left for Vienna, where he met — or so went the rumors — with a number of members of Parliament and they were by his side wherever he went.

What sort of important negotiations he had with them it was impossible to unearth, but he apparently had his fingers in a new proposal to amend the law on mining rights.

There was something new about it in the papers every day — arguments pro and con — and it looked entirely possible that before long a law would be adopted to permit mining even in the city center, though only in exceptional cases, of course.

There was something strange about the whole thing, and public opinion had it that some big coal firm must be lurking in the background.

After all, Mackintosh alone couldn't be interested in that. Most likely he was just a front man for some consortium.

In any case, he soon returned to Prague, and in a fine mood at that. No one had ever seen him so patient.

"And why not, he's doing well. Just yesterday he bought another piece of real estate — that's number thirteen now," said the Land Registry's Chief Comptroller at the clerks' table in the casino. "You know it, that place on the corner, the Doubtful Virgin, kitty-corner from the Three Iron Ninnies, which at present is the Chief City Finder's Commission of the District Flood Overseer."

"That man will out-speculate himself yet," said the Construction Councillor, "and gentlemen, do you know what his latest request is? He wants to tear down three of his buildings: the one on Perlová Street — the fourth one on the right next to the Powder Tower — and *numero conscriptionis* 47184/ii. The new building permits have already been approved!"

Everyone stood frozen, mouths open wide in amazement.

The autumn wind howled through the streets. Nature was taking a deep breath before bedding down for the winter.

The skies were so blue and cold, the clouds so plump and imposing, it was as if the Lord himself had commissioned a painting from Master Wilhelm Schulz.

O, how clean and splendid the city would be had not that vile American, in his destructive fury, poisoned the clear air with the fine dust of old masonry. How could anyone have approved such a thing!

Tearing down three buildings, well, that's one thing, but all thirteen at once? That's taking it too far.

People coughing everywhere you look, and the pain when that damned brick dust gets in your eyes.

"I don't want to see what kinds of crazy things he's going to put up instead. Art nouveau, no doubt — I'd bet anything on that." So went the talk in the street.

"You must have heard wrong, Mr. Šebor! What? He doesn't plan to put up anything at all? Has he lost his mind? What did he submit those new blueprints for then?"

"Simple, so they'd grant him a preliminary permit to wreck his buildings!"

"Gentlemen, have you heard the latest news?" Castle Construction Apprentice Vyskočil was quite out of breath. "There's gold in this city. Yes indeed! Gold! Perhaps even right here, under our feet."

They all looked down at the feet of Lord Vyskočil, as long and flat as sponge cakes in his patent leather shoes.

All of Příkopy Street rushed over to join in.

"Did I hear someone talk about gold?" shouted Löwenstein the Commercial Councillor.

"I hear Mr. Mackintosh found some soil with gold in it in the land under his building on Perlová Street," an official from the Mining Bureau confirmed. "They've even telegraphed to bring in a commission from Vienna."

Within a few days George Mackintosh had become the biggest celebrity in town. His photograph — with his sharply chiseled profile and a mocking expression on his thin lips — hung in every shop window.

The newspapers carried his biography, and all of a sudden the sports correspondents knew his exact weight, the measurements of his chest and biceps, even his lung capacity.

It was no trouble at all to obtain an interview with him.

He was back in the Red Sun Hotel, granting audiences to all, proffering rare cigars and recounting with delightful grace what had brought him to knock down his buildings and mine for gold in the foundations left behind:

His new device, the fruit of his very own brain, gave the precise location of gold under the earth according to fluctuations in electric current. He had conducted a series of searches by night, not only in the cellars of his own buildings, but also, after negotiating in secret to arrange access, in the cellars of all the neighboring buildings as well.

"What you see here are the official reports of the Mining Bureau as well as the expert evaluation of Professor Senkrecht from Vienna, an outstanding specialist and, by the way, a very close and long-standing friend of mine."

And indeed, there it stood, in black and white and certified with an official seal: gold on every single one of the construction sites American George Mackintosh had purchased; gold, in its common form, mixed with sand in such a high proportion that one could safely predict the presence of an immense quantity of the precious metal, particularly in the substrata.

This type of find, said the reports, had previously been known only in America and in Asia. Nevertheless, they went on, one could concur with the opinion of Mr. Mackintosh that this site was apparently a riverbed dating from prehistoric times. It would be impossible, of course, to calculate the worth of the find with any precision, but the wealth of metal concealed here was certainly of first-class rank, perhaps even entirely unprecedented.

Of particular interest was the plan the American had proposed for the expansion of the gold mines, which had won full approval from an expert commission.

From this plan it was evident that the former riverbed, which started at one of the American's buildings, wound through a series of complicated twists and turns beneath the neighboring homes to his other holdings before disappearing again into the earth at one of Mackintosh's corner houses on Celetná Street.

The proof that this was so and could not be otherwise was so simple and clear that everyone had to grasp it, even if they didn't believe in the reliability of the electric-powered metal detector.

What luck that the new mining law was now in effect!

How prudent and discreet the American had been to arrange it all beforehand!

The landlords whose lots had been suddenly found to contain such wealth now swaggered about the city's coffeehouses, praising to the skies their shrewd neighbor, who had once been so groundlessly and shamefully slandered.

"The shame of those libelers!"

Each evening these gentlemen would hold long meetings before gathering in a small committee to take council with their lawyer about what their next move should be.

"It couldn't be simpler! We'll do everything precisely the way Mr. Mackintosh did," said the lawyer. "Submit any old blueprints as the law requires, and then boom, boom, boom, so we can reach the foundations as quickly as possible. There's no other way to do it, as digging in the cellars now would be useless, and, for that matter, under section 47 subsection Y slash XXIII, it is impermissible."

And so it happened.

The suggestion of the sophisticated foreign engineer that they first make sure Mackintosh had not secretly transported the gold-bearing sand to the site in order to lead the commission astray was dismissed by all with knowing smiles.

The pounding and hammering in the streets, the falling beams, the shouting workers, the clamor of carts full of rubble, and to top it all off, that damned wind driving those thick clouds of dust all around — it was enough to drive anyone mad!

All of the city was suffering from conjunctivitis, eye clinic waiting rooms were filled to near bursting with patients, and Professor Pisálek's new brochure "On the Detrimental Effects of Modern Construction on the Human Cornea" was sold out within a matter of days.

It grew worse and worse with each passing hour.

Traffic was tied up in knots. People surrounded the Red Sun in droves and everyone wanted to speak with the American to find out if he thought there might also be gold under other homes besides those indicated in his plan.

Military patrols walked the city, official declarations were posted at every intersection announcing the strictest prohibition on tearing down any more buildings without the permission of the ministry.

The police went about with weapons unsheathed, which scarcely helped the situation.

There were some dreadful cases of mental disturbance: in the middle of the night one widow crawled up on the roof of her house on the outskirts of town in her nightgown and, with piercing shrieks, tore the shingles from her roof.

Young mothers roamed the streets like drunkards while their poor forsaken newborns perished of thirst, forgotten in their cribs.

A dark haze hung over the city. It was as if the demon of gold had spread its bat-like wings and blocked out the sun.

At last, the big day arrived. Once-splendid edifices had since vanished as if plucked from the soil, and an army of miners stepped in where once walls had stood.

The shovels and pickaxes flew.

And the gold? Not even a trace! It must be deeper than they had assumed.

Then — what have we here? A special oversized advertisement in the papers:

> From George Mackintosh to his dear friends and his dearly beloved city! Circumstances oblige me to bid farewell forever to you all.
>
> I hereby dedicate to the city one large air balloon which you will see launched today for the first time from Josef Square. In my memory, you may use it at any time free of charge. As I did not have time to stop by to say good-bye to all the gentlemen in town, I am leaving the city a large calling card. . . .

"He must have lost his marbles!"

Leaving a calling card to the city! Utter nonsense!

"What is all this supposed to mean? Can you make any sense of it?" So went the talk around town.

"The only thing that doesn't fit is that the American went and sold all of his building lots a week ago in secret!"

It was Maloch, the photographer, who finally solved the puzzle. He was the first to climb aboard and take a ride in the celebrated balloon, and he took a picture of the devastated city from a bird's-eye view.

Now the photo was hanging in his shop window and the street was crowded with people who wanted to get a look.

What did it show?

Shining out of the dark sea of homes through the white ruins, the vacant lots and demolished homes linked to form a snarled message:

G M

The American's initials!

Most of the landlords had a heart attack, except for old Mr. Schlüsselbein, the Commercial Councillor, who didn't give a hoot since his house had been on the verge of collapse anyway.

He just rubbed his irritated eyes in annoyance and grumbled, "I always said that Mackintosh never did have a head for anything serious."

Translated from the Czech by Alex Zucker

The Hotel Pařίž

Bohumil Hrabal

THE HOTEL PAŘÍŽ was so beautiful it almost
knocked me over. So many mirrors and brass balustrades
and brass door handles and brass candelabras, all polished
till the place shone like a place of gold. There were red carpets and glass doors everywhere, just like in a château. Mr.
Brandejs gave me a warm welcome and took me to my temporary quarters, a little room in the attic with such a pretty
view of Prague that I decided, because of the room and the
view, to try to stay there permanently. After I'd unpacked my
suitcase to hang out my tuxedo and my underwear, I opened
a closet and saw it was full of suits, and a second closet was
full of umbrellas, and a third was full of topcoats, and inside,
hanging on strings nailed to the wall, were hundreds of ties.
I pushed the hangers together and hung up my clothes and
then looked out over the rooftops of Prague, and when I saw
the shimmering castle, the home of Czech kings, I was
flooded with tears and forgot all about the Hotel Tichota.

When I went downstairs, it was noon, and the waiters
were changing shifts and having lunch, and I saw they were
eating croquettes — boiled potato croquettes with fried bread
crumbs — and everyone in the kitchen was served this, including the boss, who was eating in the kitchen just like the
cashier. Only the chef de cuisine and his assistants had boiled

From *I Served the King of England.*

potatoes in their skins. I was served croquettes with bread crumbs too. The boss had me sit down beside him, and while I ate, he ate too, but rather delicately, as if to say: If I, the owner, can eat this, then you, my employees, can eat it too. Soon he wiped his mouth with a napkin and took me out into the restaurant. My first job was to serve the beer, so I picked up the full glasses in the taproom and arranged them on my tray, putting a red glass token in a box for each beer, which was how they kept track of them here, and the old waiter pointed with his chin to where I was supposed to take the beer. From then on he just used his eyes, and I never made a mistake. Within an hour I could tell the old head-waiter was stroking me with his eyes, letting me know he liked me. He was class itself, a real movie actor, born to the tuxedo. I'd never seen anyone look better in a formal suit, and he seemed right at home in this hall of mirrors. Even though it was afternoon, all the lights were on, candle-shaped lamps with a bulb in every one and cut-glass crystal pendants everywhere. When I saw myself in the mirror carrying the bright Pilsener beer, I seemed different somehow. I saw that I'd have to stop thinking of myself as small and ugly. The tuxedo looked good on me here, and when I stood beside the headwaiter, who had curly gray hair that looked as though a hairdresser had done it, I could also see in the mirror that all I really wanted was to work right here at this station with this headwaiter, who radiated serenity, who knew everything there was to know, who paid close attention to everything, who filled orders and was always smiling as though he were at a dance or hosting a ball in his own home. He also knew which tables were still waiting for their food and would see that they got it, and he knew who wanted to pay, though I

never saw anyone raise his hand and snap his fingers or shake
the bill. The headwaiter would gaze out over the restaurant
as if he were surveying a vast crowd of people, or looking out
over the countryside from an observation tower, or scanning
the sea from the pilothouse of a steamship, or not looking at
anything, and every movement a guest made told him at
once what that guest wanted. I noticed right away that the
headwaiter didn't like one waiter and would reproach him
with his eyes for getting the plates mixed up and taking the
port to table eleven instead of table six.

When I'd been serving beer for a week, I noticed that
whenever this particular waiter brought the food from the
kitchen on a tray he would stop before he went through the
swinging door and, when he thought no one was looking,
lower the tray from the level of his eyes to the level of his
heart, look hungrily at the food, and take a pinch of this and
a pinch of that — just a tiny amount each time so it looked as
if he'd accidentally dipped his finger in the food and was
licking it off. I saw the headwaiter catch him at it but say
nothing, just watch. Then the waiter would wave his hand,
hoist the tray over his shoulder, kick open the door, and rush
into the restaurant. He always ran as though the tray were
falling forward, his legs a-flurry, but it was a fact that no one
else dared carry as many plates as Karel (that was his name).
He could get twenty plates on his tray and lay eight along his
outstretched arm as if it were a narrow table, and hold two
more in his outspread fingers, and three plates in the other
hand. It was almost like a vaudeville routine, and I suspect
that Brandejs, the boss, liked the waiter and thought that the
way he served the food was one of the attractions of the establishment. So almost every day we employees had potato
croquettes for lunch, sometimes with poppy seed, sometimes

with a sauce, or with a toasted roll or covered with butter and sugar, or with raspberry syrup or with chopped parsley and melted lard. Each time, there would be the boss himself, eating those potato croquettes with us in the kitchen. He never ate very much, because he said he was on a diet. But at two o'clock Karel the waiter would bring him a tray, and judging by the silver covers over the food, it must have been a small goose or a chicken or a duck, or some kind of game, whatever was in season. He always had it brought into one of the private chambers, to make it look as though it were for someone else, a member or a broker from the Fruit and Vegetable Exchange, because the brokers always went on conducting their business after hours in the Hotel Paříž. But when no one was looking, our boss would slip into the room, and when he came out he'd be glowing with satisfaction, a toothpick stuck in the corner of his mouth. I suspect that Karel the waiter had some kind of arrangement with the boss. When the main day at the exchange, which was Thursday, was over, the brokers would come to our hotel to celebrate over champagne and cognac the deal they'd closed. On each table would be trays laden with food, or really only one tray, but full enough to make it a real feast, and every Thursday, from eleven o'clock in the morning on, some brightly painted young ladies would be sitting in the restaurant, the kind I'd met at Paradise's when I was working at the Golden City of Prague, and they'd be smoking and drinking vermouth and waiting for the brokers to show up. When the brokers did show up, the girls would split up and go to separate tables, and the men would select them for the private chambers. Then I could hear the sounds of laughter and the tinkling of glasses through the curtains as I walked past, and this would go on for hours, until finally the brokers would leave in high spirits and the young ladies would come out and comb their hair, redo their kiss-smeared lipstick, tuck in their blouses, and glance behind them, almost putting their necks out of joint trying to see if the stocking they'd just put back on had the line, the seam, running straight down the middle of their legs into their shoes to the exact center of their heels. When the brokers left, neither I nor anyone else was ever allowed to go into the private chambers, and we all knew why. Several times, through a half-drawn curtain, I saw Karel lifting the cushions, and that was his little business on the side, picking up lost coins and bills, and the occasional ring or watch chain. It was all his, the money that fell out of the pockets of the brokers' trousers, coats, and vests as they dressed or undressed or were writhing about.

One morning Karel loaded up his tray with twelve main dishes and as usual stopped just inside the door to pinch a bit of sirloin tip and a touch of Brussels sprouts to go along with it, topping it off with a morsel of dressing from the veal. Then he lifted the tray as if the food had given him new strength, and with a smile on his face struck out into the restaurant. But a customer who was taking snuff, or had a cold, inhaled abruptly through his nose, and as he inhaled it was as if the force of the intake pulled him straight up by the hair, because he suddenly rose to his feet, sneezing loudly, and caught the corner of the tray with his shoulder. Karel, leaning forward at the waist, had to run to catch up to the loaded tray, which now was sailing through the air like a flying carpet, because Karel always carried his food high. Either the tray was too fast or Karel's legs were too slow, but in any case when he reached for it the tray slipped away from his upturned hand, his finger scrabbling desperately for it as all of us in the business watched, including the boss, who was entertaining a group from the Hotel Owners' Association. Mr. Šroubek himself was at the banquet table, and he saw what then happened just as we had foreseen it would. Karel took one more mighty leap in the air and managed to catch the tray before it fell, but two plates slipped off one after the other, and first pieces of beef roll à la Puzsta, then dumplings poured over a guest who was just raising his eyes from the menu to ask if the meat was tender and the sauce warm enough and the dumplings light. It all slid off the plates and onto the guest, and as he rose to his feet dripping with sauce, the beef roll à la Puzsta and the dumplings tumbled off his lap and fell under the table. One dumpling remained on his head like a small cap, a yarmulke, the kind a rabbi wears, or a priest's biretta. When Karel, who had managed to save all the other ten plates, saw that and saw Mr. Šroubek, who owned the Hotel Šroubek, he raised the tray even higher, gave it a little toss, flipped it over, and flung all ten plates onto the carpet, demonstrating, as if he were in a play or a pantomime, how disgusted he felt about those two plates. He undid his apron just as theatrically, flung it on the floor, and stomped out in a fury, then changed into his street clothes and went out to get drunk. I didn't understand it yet, but everyone in the business said that if you dropped the two plates like that, the other ten had to end up on the floor too, because for a waiter it was a question of honor. But the matter was far from over. Karel came back, his eyes flashing, and sat down in the kitchen, glowering out into the restaurant. Suddenly he jumped up and tried to pull the large cupboard down on himself, the one that held all the glasses. The cashier and the cook rushed over and pushed the cupboard back upright, while the glasses clattered out of it and crashed to the floor, but those two plates had given Karel such power that he almost managed to pull the cupboard over three times. Each time the cooks, who by now were all red in the face, slowly pushed it back upright, and just when everyone had got his breath back, Karel jumped up and grabbed the kitchen stove — which was so long that when you added wood at one end, the fire would almost be out by the time you got to the oven at the other — and gave the stove such a yank that he pulled the stovepipe out of the wall, and soon the kitchen was full of smoke and fumes and everyone was choking. With great effort they got the pipe back in place, and the cooks, all smeared with soot, collapsed in their chairs and looked about to see where Karel was, but he was gone. Just as we all heaved sighs of relief, suddenly we heard a tinkling sound. Karel had kicked a hole in the glass of the air shaft over the stove and smashed his way down into the kitchen, and he landed with one leg up to his knee in the lunchtime special, which was tripe soup, and the other leg in a pot of goulash combined with sauce for the filet-on-mushrooms. There were splinters of glass everywhere, so the cooks gave up, and they ran for the porter, who was a former wrestler, to take Karel out by force, since they decided he must have some kind of grudge against the Hotel Paříž. The porter set his legs firmly apart and spread his huge paws as though he were holding a skein of wool to be wound into a ball and said, What's it going to be, you horse's ass? But Karel slugged the porter so hard that the porter fell over, and the police had to be called in. By the time the police arrived Karel was docile, but in the corridor on the way out he knocked down two of them and kicked a dent in the helmet of a third while the policeman was still wearing it. So they dragged him into one of the private rooms and beat him up, and each time he screamed, all the guests in the restaurant looked at one another and shrugged their shoulders. Finally the policemen took him out, all bruised up, but as he passed the cloakroom he told the girl that those two plates would cost some more yet, and he was right, because word had barely come back that he'd settled down when he suddenly kicked a hole in the porcelain sink and yanked the pipes out of the wall so that everything in the room, including the policemen, was soaking wet before they managed to stop up the holes with their fingers.

And so I became a waiter on the floor under the guidance of the headwaiter Mr. Skřivánek. . . .

Now it was I who served the brokers every Thursday, because Karel never came back. Like all rich people, the brokers were as cheerful and playful as puppies, and when they closed a deal they would throw their money around like butchers who'd won at cards. Of course, butchers who played cards would occasionally lose their shirts and get home three days later minus their buggy, minus their horses, minus the livestock they'd bought, with nothing left but a whip. Sometimes these brokers would lose everything too, and then they'd sit in the private chambers looking at the world like Jeremiah watching Jerusalem burn. Gradually I gained the confidence of the young ladies who waited in the cafe until the exchange closed and then went down to the private chambers, and it didn't matter whether it was eleven in the morning or late afternoon or dusk or late at night, because at the Hotel Paříž the lights were always on, like a

chandelier you'd forgotten to switch off. Best of all I liked
the private chambers the young ladies called the Clinic, or
Diagnostics 100, or the Department of Internal Medicine.
The brokers who were still at the height of their virility
would try to get the women tipsy as fast as possible, then
slowly remove their blouses and skirts until they were rolling
around with them on the upholstered couches and chairs as
naked as God made them, and the brokers would end up
completely worn out, so exhausted from making love in unusual positions that they looked as if they'd just suffered a
heart attack. But in the Department of Internal Medicine or
Diagnostics 100 things were merrier. Entertaining the older
gentlemen was the most popular job, because this was where
the girls raked in the most. The older brokers would laugh
and make jokes and treat the undressing of a young woman
as a collective game of strip poker, removing her clothes little
by little, right on the table, while they sipped their drinks
from their crystal champagne glasses and savored the bouquet. The girl would then lie back on the table and the old
brokers would gather around her with their glasses and
plates of caviar and lettuce and sliced Hungarian salami, and
they'd put on their spectacles and study every fold and curve
of her beautiful female body, and then, as if they were at a
fashion show or a life-study class in some academy of art,
they'd ask the girl to sit, or stand up, or kneel, or let her legs
dangle from the table and swing back and forth as though
she were washing them in a stream. These brokers would
never worry or argue among themselves about who had what
part of her body closest to them, but their animation was
like the animation of a painter transferring what excites him
in a landscape to his canvas, and so these old men would
peer through their glasses at the crook of an elbow, a strand

of loose hair, an instep, an ankle, a lap, and one would gently part the two beautiful cheeks of her behind and gaze with childish admiration at what was revealed, and another would shriek in delight and roll his eyes to the ceiling, as if thanking the Lord Himself for the privilege of peering between the open thighs of a young woman and touching whatever pleased him most with his fingers or his lips. This private chamber was always filled with light, not only with the strong light from the ceiling funneling down through a parchment lampshade but also with the glitter of wineglasses and four pairs of spectacle lenses moving back and forth like tiny veiled fish in an illuminated aquarium. When they had had their fill of looking, the brokers would call it quits and pour the young woman some champagne, and she would sit on the table and drink toasts with them, and they would call her by her first name, and she would help herself to anything she wanted from the table. The older men made jokes and were courteous to her, while from the other chambers you could hear raucous laughter, sometimes suddenly silenced, and I often felt the urge to barge in there, certain I'd find a dead body or a dying broker lying on the floor. Then the old men would dress her just the way they had undressed her, with none of the apathy that comes afterward, none of the indifference, but with the same courtesy they had shown her from the start. When they left, one of them would always pay the whole bill, they would tip the headwaiter and I always got a hundred crowns, and they would leave, glowing and at peace with themselves, full of beautiful images that would last them a week. By next Monday they would be looking forward to examining a different woman on Thursday, because they never had the same woman twice, perhaps in order to spread their reputation among the Prague prostitutes. At the end of each session, the young woman they had just examined would hang around the private chamber, waiting, breathing heavily and eyeing me greedily as if I were a movie actor, because she was so aroused she couldn't bring herself to leave. So after I finished clearing the table and put away the last piece of cutlery, I'd have to finish what the old men began. The women would throw themselves on me with such passion and eagerness, it was as if they were doing it for the first time, and for those few minutes I felt tall and handsome and curly-haired, and I knew that I was king for those beautiful young women, though it was only because their bodies had been so tickled by eyes, hands, and tongues that they could scarcely walk. Not until I felt them climaxing once, twice, would they come to life again, their eyes would return, the glassy absent stare of passion would disappear, and they would see things normally again. Once more I became a tiny waiter, standing in for someone strong and handsome, performing on command every Thursday with increasing appetite and skill. This had been the specialty of Karel, my predecessor, who had the aptitude and the capacity and the love for it, though I had that too. And I must have been good in other ways as well, because all the young women would greet me when they met me in the hotel or on the street, and if they were a long way off they'd bob or wave their hankies or their purses, and if they had nothing in their hands, they'd at least give me a friendly wave, and I'd bow or acknowledge them with a wide sweep of my hat, then stand straight again and raise my chin, feeling taller than my double-soled shoes could make me.

Translated from the Czech by Paul Wilson

The Case of the Washerwoman

Egon Erwin Kisch

AT FIVE O'CLOCK in the afternoon Frau Bergman was found dead in her apartment. She had been murdered and robbed. Suspicion was immediately cast on her maid's lover, whom the concierge had seen leaving the house at about three o'clock that afternoon. By six o'clock the maid, as well as Franz Polanski, her lover, had been turned over to the police.

Instead of waiting at the station for the end of the preliminary investigation, I rushed off to the home of the accused. Officers had already been there, searched through Franz Polanski's effects, and tried to draw information from his mother. But the news of her son's arrest had thrown the old woman into such a state of mental chaos that the officers merely summoned her to appear at the police station the following day.

When I knocked, no one answered. I entered. Frau Polanski was sitting all alone in her room and did not reply to my greeting. Her eyes were moist, but she was not crying.

"I beg your pardon, Frau Polanski . . . I'm from the newspaper."

"The newspaper!" she repeated. "You can't mean it's going to be in the papers! No, not that! For heaven's sake! Think of my poor husband — dead and gone now these eighteen years — what would he say? He never had anything to do with the police in his life. Look mister, please, I'm just a poor washerwoman. I've been washing clothes over that tub for twenty-five years and never once has there been so much as a diaper missing. I've never even mixed up a pair of stockings. No one watches out like I do to see that sleeves don't get frayed. And now I'm to be in the papers where everyone can read about me. Please, you wouldn't have the heart."

I tried to explain to her that it was not in my power to prevent such events from being reported. The papers were bound to print reports about burglary and murder. The words "burglary and murder" completely crushed the poor woman. She stared into the corner of the room and began to speak to herself, almost without moving her lips. "Murder . . . burglary. Naturally. It must be in the papers. I hadn't thought of that at all. And my Franz is a thief and a murderer. Yes, Franz Polanski, son of Anna Polanski, laundress, Number 4 Mostecká Street, a thief and a murderer. Now the whole neighborhood will read about my shame."

"No one will think of blaming you, Frau Polanski. Everyone knows you've been a hardworking, honest woman."

But she paid no attention to my words and kept repeating dully, "A murderer! A thief!"

"How long has your son been going around with Frau Bergmann's maid? How long has he been out of work?"

"Murderer. Thief. Franz Polanski, the son of Anna Polanski . . ."

I was plainly wasting my time. I made to leave, saying that I had had no intention of bothering her, that I had only thought she might be able to help her son if she could tell me more about it.

"Help him? How can anyone help him? I'm just a poor washerwoman."

I explained to her that there were mitigating circumstances in every case. For example, a person in great need might be excused for doing almost anything. Or perhaps it could be proved that Franz was not altogether in his right mind. Perhaps he suffered from spells of one kind or another. The court would also take hereditary factors into consideration, for example, if the man's father or mother suffered from fits of sudden anger.

"Hereditary?" she cried. "You mean like a person gets a disease from his mother?"

"Please, Frau Polanski. I had no intention of insulting you, what I meant was merely that — "

"But it's true! He got it from me. It's not his fault. My poor Franz. He inherited it from me. Yes, from me!"

I could see where this new tack was leading. The woman thought she saw a way out for her Franz by taking all the blame upon herself, perhaps by presenting herself as a regular Borgia.

"Yes, you're right, I can help him! You've got to believe me when I tell you this murder was my fault. I carried it around inside me all my life. I never told a single soul, not even in confession, as often as I've gone, but I'll tell it to you and you can put it in your paper. Let the police come and arrest me. Let the neighbors point at me. All I want is to help my boy. It's hereditary, that's all it is. The truth is, I'm a murderer."

I could smell what was coming. She was going to dig up a few miserable infractions and in the end the whole business wouldn't be worth a stick of type.

"Yes, I'm a murderer. Only my boy had more strength than I had. He went through with it. I didn't."

"We often have ideas like that run through our heads."

"No, no, I'm not talking of anything that just runs through your head. Let me show you something."

Frau Polanski tore off her kerchief so that her hair fell in disarray over her forehead. She hurried over to a table, suddenly seeming like a much younger woman. She yanked open the drawer and took out a kitchen knife.

"See this knife? I tried to stab a man to death with this once. That's a long time ago, thirty years ago, when I was parlor maid at Martin's, the tax assessor, in Marianská Street. I was a young girl then, just in from the farm."

"Who did you try to stab?"

"The first man who had ever been nice to me in my whole life! No one had ever been nice to me before. At home there were eight of us and we never heard a kind word from our parents. And then along comes someone who says to me, 'You're a nice kid,' and he pets me and kisses me and first thing you know I've given myself to him."

"And of course he didn't marry you. The old story."

"Go on. I never even thought of marriage. After all, he was Madam's brother. It's like when you take clothes and soak them in suds and then you can twist them between your fingers and do anything you want with them. That's just the way he handled me with his flatteries. Of course, you can go too far and wash the color and the nap out of the laundry, and it's the same with people . . ."

Very well put, I thought to myself and, taking out my notebook, I wrote down: "Philosophy over a Washboard." Make a good heading over a double-columned piece.

"And for that you wanted to kill him?"

"Oh, no. I was such a goose. I thought that's the way it has to be. But then something happened that opened my eyes. He told me to come to his house one evening and wear the blue blouse he'd bought me because he was going to have a little celebration. So I got permission to go and went off feeling very happy. He had two gentlemen friends with him, and he had me sit down at the table between them, and next to him sat a lady — well, a *lady!* I saw right off what kind of a lady she was. Just the kind of a hussy he was cut out for."

"I can well imagine," I nodded.

"We had sandwiches and wine and then someone blew out the lights. Just the table lamp with a red silk shade was still lit. His two friends began to get very attentive and kept telling me to drink more, and my Madam's brother kept saying to go ahead, this wasn't the Sunday school back home. I felt so strange. After all, I didn't want to be the one to spoil the party and get him angry, so I just played along. Then one of the men said the girls should get undressed. The other one was all for it, but I couldn't bring myself to do it. So he took me to one side and told me I ought to be ashamed of myself, said I hadn't been so hoity-toity before and if I didn't want to cooperate I'd better go home because he was through with me. I felt so hurt I wanted to run away."

"Did you?"

"No. The door was locked. So I drank a lot of brandy and wine to brace myself, and those dirty pigs took my clothes off. The other one slipped out of her clothes all by herself, but of course she had on fine cambric underthings with real lace and she wanted to show off. I was ashamed of my long cotton underdrawers. Nothing in the world could have made me take them down — and I was a lot prettier than she was."

A few minutes ago I had been in a room smelling of soapsuds, in the company of a weepy old washerwoman, with a washtub and a gas range, and two religious pictures on the wall. Now all that had vanished. Around me was the dim red light of a bachelor's apartment and in front of me a young girl who had been forced to undress.

"And then they turned out the last light. In the morning

my two new lovers took me home in a carriage. I was vomiting and couldn't think straight. When I got to the kitchen, I could hardly stand up. I was feverish and of course Madam snarled at me. 'Oh, I know, it's not so easy to work after making a jolly night of it,' she says, 'with drinking and heaven knows what kind of gay carryings-on.' She told me to pack my things and get out by the first of the month. Something just boiled up inside of me. Maybe it was the devil in me, but when that brother of hers came for dinner, I was completely out of my mind, and I took this kitchen knife, this very one, and I went for him and stuck it into him."

Now she did look like Lucrezia Borgia.

"I tried to stab him in the heart, but maybe he dodged, or maybe the blade glanced off his wallet or something. Anyhow, all the knife did was cut him deep in the arm so the blood began to spurt out all over."

"Did they call the police?"

"Not they! They took good care not to call in the police. But the whole family piled on me and held me down. Then I fainted and they had to carry me to my bed. Next morning, sick as I was, I packed my few belongings in my little wooden trunk and left. But I took the kitchen knife with me as a souvenir, and I left the blue blouse my lover had given me behind. Go ahead, write it all down, young man, and put it into your paper. Frau Polanski is an evil murderer, only she didn't have the strength to go through with it. Franz Polanski is completely innocent. He's just a victim, heir to the blood of Frau Polanski and her murders. Write that down."

"Murders? You mean you tried it a second time?"

"Of course I did. I'm guilty of two murders for which I had neither the strength nor the time. There in that washtub, that's where all my strength is, buried and drowned, and all my time too." She drummed her fingers against the sides of the tub. "This is my cradle and my bed and my coffin. My whole life is in that tub, washing cambric and silk and linen and all sorts of fine things that don't belong to me. I've never stopped envying the women who wear them, because I too was once young and pretty."

A youthful hatred seemed to well up in her. "How I longed to wear those delicate underthings, but I would just clench my fists and — " she laughed convulsively and struck at the wooden tub.

"I used to sneak a pair of lace stockings and a fine cambric chemise out of the laundry now and then, but that was long ago, awfully long ago.

"I had a friend on the police force," she went on, "and was he the jealous one! I couldn't even dance with anyone else. But one day I found myself pregnant and he told me he was just an auxiliary policeman and couldn't think of getting married and so I just couldn't have the child. I listened to all kinds of advice and drank oceans of hot claret and ate tons of cloves, but nothing would help. So he talked me into sleeping with Polanski and then blaming it on him."

So now the dead husband too was to be drawn into this pointless self-accusation.

"Don't go, young man. Now comes the real murder story, the kind your paper will print. Polanski was a steady and respectable fellow who was a porter in a store on our street. He always brought me flowers and blushed whenever he saw me. At first I wouldn't hear of it but my fine policeman friend talked at me till I was deaf and dumb. One evening I went home from the dance hall with Polanski. My friend followed me right to the door to make sure I wouldn't change my mind. I felt sick to my stomach like the other time, and I was filled with such a hate that on my next date with the policeman I took my knife along. This time I was very clear and cold and I knew my knife wouldn't slip . . ."

"But you didn't really —"

"No, I didn't kill him. I didn't even stab him, for the simple reason that he never showed up. Once he'd got me in bed with another man he no longer felt any responsibility for me. A real man of honor. For a long time I didn't have the courage to say right out to Polanski, 'I'm pregnant.' But when it was plain as the nose on your face, I finally came out with it. I decided I'd get rid of my child, even if it cost my life. But there wasn't a midwife anywhere who would do it for me because by this time I was seven months gone. I drank more hot claret, and jumped from the table twenty times, and I knelt for hours before the Mother of God and prayed and confessed and fasted and made vows, but nothing helped. On this devil's own wall, this tub, I pressed my belly and washed away with clenched fists, washed chemises that were bloody all right, but not a drop of blood could I squeeze out of me. Then I took out that old knife again and I stabbed myself in the belly, to start the blood flowing, to kill the child and myself too —

"They took me to the hospital where I lay for twelve days in a fever. When I came to myself, they showed me my child, my little Franz. The knife hadn't even grazed him. And perhaps it was all for the best because I soon came to love him. I even got to love Polanski, who sat all day long at my bedside and then married me. He had only one fear — that the boy might have got something from my blood, my blood that wouldn't flow without a knife. But I'll tell everything to the judge, just as I told it to you, and I won't beat around the bush. I'll tell them — "

Just then the door was jerked open. "Good evening, Mother."

Frau Polanski looked at her son, who strode in and tossed his cap on the bed. She was not quite herself yet; she was still somewhere else, standing before the judge.

"D'you know I was arrested for murder? And for burglary? What do you think of that, Mother?" He noticed the ransacked drawers. "So they've been here too, those smart cops."

Frau Polanski stared at her son with wide-open, unbelieving eyes.

"What's wrong, Mother? You look as if you really thought I'd smashed in old Frau Bergmann's skull!"

"Excuse me, but I'm a reporter," I said. "Why were you released?"

Franz Polanski laughed out loud. "Well, what do you know, Mother, I'm going to be in the papers after all. They've caught the real murderer. He's the son of the concierge. But I haven't had a bite to eat since noon. I'm starving."

She looked at me and I could read her thoughts. A moment ago she had been the mother of a murderer and she had bared the darkest recesses of her life to a reporter. Now, suddenly, she was no longer the mother of a murderer, and this man from the papers had nothing more to do in her honest home.

"Mother, don't you hear me? I haven't had a bite since noon! Why do you keep staring that way? Come on, let's eat."

Frau Polanski gathered herself together. She tied her kerchief over her head and became an old washerwoman once more, bent and humble. "All right, all right, son," she said as she went over to the kitchen stove. "Don't rush me."

I left without a story.

Translated from the German by Guy Endore

The Magic Flute

Bohumil Hrabal

THE GODS HAVE ABANDONED this land, the antique heroes have left too, Heracles and Prometheus. . . . My wife decided to leave, and so did Perla, daughter of the Bratislava rabbi who loved me and I loved her because she resembled my Pipsi. This Sunday evening a bloody sun was setting over Prague and a cinnamon sky in the west presaged heavy winds, the Old Town Square was ringed tight by huge yellow police vans with barred windows, in Kaprova Street water cannons were blasting pedestrians and sweeping them under the wheels of cars, in a passageway people were trying to recover from beatings they had just received, an eighty-year-old woman was shouting: who will pay for this soaked coat of mine? A group of militiamen stood in front of the Industrial Arts College demanding entrance. . . . People huddled in the subway passages were weeping, overcome not by emotion but by tear gas . . . the police began to arrest everybody with drenched clothing, I sat down at Otto's because the Myrtle Tavern was closed owing to technical difficulties, a young man in a green sweater pulled up a chair next to me, then three more came and sat down at the next table, all of them were young policemen dressed for duty in windbreakers and colorful sweaters, they looked like football players, we sniffed each other out with our eyes and I was scared, I stared into the very heart of silence because the gods had abandoned this world and this town, this Sunday evening I finally reached the peak of loud solitude and the pinnacle of emptiness, I reached final disquiet, the point achieved by Kierkegaard and Friedrich Nietzsche. How many times have I wanted to jump from my fifth floor window, not for the reasons I've just given but because I had to watch my Pipsi dying, my wife that looked so much like Perla, but when I learned that Kafka had wanted to jump from the fifth floor of the Maison Oppelt, house of the wine merchants who stored seven hundred thousand bottles of rare wines under the Old Town Square, when I read that Malte Laurids Brigge in Paris had also lived on the fifth floor, when I learned about all those fifth floors, I postponed my jump. If I had the strength I'd buy a can of gasoline and set myself on fire, but I am afraid, I am not brave, I am not like Gaius Marcus Scaevolla, the young Roman condemned to die at the stake, who put his right arm into the blaze in front of the terrified gaze of his enemies, remarking that Rome had thousands of men of equal courage, but I am afraid, as a matter of fact I like to be afraid for I am full of a terminal disquiet like Kierkegaard, like Nietzsche, my eyes are full of tears and I am drenched like those who tasted tear gas with their own eyes and felt the shock of water cannons with their own bodies, I feel these things, I feel what others experience with their bodies and souls thanks to the power of fantasy and tactile imagination. . . . On Monday, when I arrived in Prague from Kersko and got out at the Museum at a quarter to four, I saw the statue of St. Wenceslas looming up menacingly in full armor, with alert-looking policemen ringing the statue, their backs to the saint's horse, young fellows with jackets pulled tight in the back so as to emphasize their chests, I saw streams of people walking by and as they passed the spot on the edge of the sidewalk where flowers were about to be laid, they stared at that spot, people were not forbidden to place flowers there but they were not permitted to do so, either. . . . I walked with my head hanging down and suddenly I became aware of girlish hands lifted in front of me, hands holding sprigs of carnations, gently, to keep the fingers from bruising the flowers, and above the flowers I saw the eyes of young women, open as wide as if they were on their way to confirmation or to a Bach mass, I walked along with one of those maidens, she stopped at the edge of the St. Wenceslas monument and followed by the gaze of onlookers she began to cross the avenue, then hesitated, but a young policeman waved her across with a mild gesture of his hand. . . .

I was ashamed that I had reached the pinnacle of emptiness and loud solitude, that I had reached terminal disquiet and was no longer any good for anything, that were I to get some sort of prize, some sort of literary award and had any kind of backbone I would at least burn the paper that stated who I was not, for if I were the person I pretend to myself to be and the person my readers take me for, I would gently take the trembling spray of flowers out of the girl's hand and place it under the hoof of St. Wenceslas's stallion . . . but I know that I no longer have the stuff for that, and therefore deserve to be mistakenly rewarded by having a water cannon blast break my backbone and a sharp needle of tear gas rip out my eyes, just as fate-crushed Oedipus tore his eyes out. . . .

What had actually taken place in this city during the last two days? The armed power of the police and the militia intervened in a crude way into the affairs of young people who had created a myth of their saint, and I believe it was those same armed units that arrogated to themselves the right to overstep the bounds of necessary force in dealing with people who had neither firearms nor stones nor sticks, who were armed only with words and whistles, who were pushing baby carriages, the situation wasn't even comparable to that of Odysseus, who had been plowing a field when his masters placed his young son in a furrow in order to force Odysseus to submit and take part in the Trojan war. . . . So what had really changed? Sooner or later tears wash the eyes clear, and eye lotion takes care of tear gas, clothes dry out or people buy new ones, arrested people will eventually be released, life will jump back into the old track. . . . Do you really believe that, Mr. Hrabal? No, sir! Those young people who took part, either actually or in spirit, they have already performed an act of commitment, of solidarity, of saying yes to a certain good, of making a pledge that will be redeemable in the future. . . .

And so I sat in the Golden Tiger, pondering over a mug the way I always do. If the gods like me I'll croak with a mug of beer in my hand. I sat there and listened to the details of that great Monday and great Sunday, those stories being told with shining eyes wove a rich carpet of reality that can no longer be erased or burned because those things had really happened and nothing of that can be unhappened. . . . I lifted my head and as always I looked up at the sky, at the sky over the church tower, it promised to be a cold, starry night, tonight I would see the sickle of the moon from my fifth-floor window, I walked down deserted Pařížská Street, a police car quietly pulled up at the curb, a man got out and began quietly placing parking tickets on the windshields of illegally parked cars, then quietly the headlights turned toward Maison Oppelt, from the fifth floor of which Franz Kafka once wanted to jump, and then I stood all alone in the square, the place was deserted, I sat down on the nearest bench and began to muse.

. . . In front of me loomed the monument to Master Jan Hus, when he was being burned at the stake an old woman brought some dry sticks so that the master could burn more easily, the monument stood in the darkness in the middle of the square whereas the Kinský Palace and its walls and the whole eastern side of the square was aglow, illuminated by sharp sodium lights in such a way that the pink and tan walls of the palaces and houses made the black silhouette of the monument stand out and as I sat by myself a youngster climbed up on the seat and began jumping from one bench to another, suddenly the soft voice of a flute sounded from the heart of the Old Town Square as if floating from a far-off meadow or a lonely lake, the voice of the flute was moving for its own sake and also because just a few hours earlier the last cars had left this square with their tear gas and their water cannons and their German shepherds, those lovely German sheepdogs that were by now probably back in their kennels resting after that strenuous Sunday and Monday . . . but here, in the Old Town Square, the voice of the flute sounded so clear from the heart of the monument that it frightened me, I got up, cupped my ear, turned my head . . . yes, now the voice of the flute grew louder, it radiated over the square and seemed to be coming from the circle of shrubs surrounding the statue of Master Jan Hus, it rose from those evergreen conifers. Several passersby crossed the square, their voices re-sounded through the emptiness but nobody stopped. Then a series of steps proceeded on a diagonal from Železná Street to Pařížská, from Dlouhá Street to Melantrichova, and then the voice of the flute stopped, the silence seemed close to bursting like an overstretched string on a violin, I saw the branches of one of the shrubs at the foot of the monument spread apart and somebody leapt out on the pavement which shone with the reflected light of the illuminated walls and then I saw a second figure separate itself from the gloom of the monument and it was a woman with a baby carriage and now a young woman and a young man stepped out of the shadows and into the sharply lit area next to the former Unicorn Pharmacy, they were pushing the carriage which perhaps contained the magic flute and I, because I am a literary type, glanced at the first-floor window of the former pharmacy and I recalled that this used to be the salon of Madame Berta Fanta, a salon where, in the old Austrian era, Franz Kafka, Albert Einstein, Rudolf Steiner, Max Brod, and Polish poets used to take part in conversations . . . and when I sat down again I realized that the magic flute sounded precisely from the region where vertical tidings unfold. . . . I believe that the government of all things will return once again to Thy hands. . . .

P.S. When I returned home I looked up the end of the third section of T. S. Eliot's *The Waste Land* and read it to the moon from the fifth floor:

> Burning burning burning burning
> O Lord Thou pluckest me out
> O Lord Thou pluckest
>
> burning

And in the notes I found that this text is from the Buddha's Fire Sermon. . . .

KERSKO, TUESDAY, JANUARY 17, 1989

Translated from the Czech by Peter Kussi

The Past

Michal Ajvaz

I'M SITTING AT THE SLÁVIA, people-watching. I recognize the pointed bird-like profile of the man in the corner who one stormy night, Malay dagger in hand, chased me past locked compartments, along empty corridors of the Orient Express. I recall his long nightshirt flashing intermittently with the lightning, the curtains fluttering through the open windows and whipping me in the face. How long ago was it? Five years, maybe ten. What was our quarrel about anyway? Something to do with rubies buried in a snowdrift in the woods, I think, or whether linguistic signs are deliberate. That woman over there, thoughtfully combing her wavy red locks, their quivering ends sparkling in the low, October afternoon sun, lived with me for seven years in a squalid house built on concrete stilts in the middle of a rotting lake surrounded on all sides by a jungle, a house with empty rooms and white walls covered with eerie maps of mold, a house where the sound of dripping water never ceased, where we whiled away the evenings on the terrace, gazing out at the water's cold surface and the darkening jungle, listening to the screeching of the beasts, and talking of the life we would live once we were back in Europe. The man arguing with the waiter at the bar is a friend from my days in Freiburg im Breisgau, the one I collaborated with on *Grundstrukturen der Wirklichkeit,* a thousand-page tome we were certain would turn philosophy on its ear and rank as the most important contribution to the field since Aristotle (as it happened, the sole copy of the manuscript was ingested by a crocodile under circumstances I can't quite recall). I see a few more faces familiar from various catacombs, Buddhist monasteries, and a night spent on the narrow, eightieth-story ledge of a sky-scraper above a sleeping city. I see faces I have known in the throes of ecstasy, eyes I have met at the bottom of the sea staring out ominously through a diving suit. But now we pre-tend not to know one another: we don't say hello; we do our best to avoid one another's eyes, though we each try to steal a glance at the other when we think the other isn't looking.

Sometimes — quite often, actually — I get into ticklish situations. Once I asked a friend to come to the Slávia after a meeting she'd had with some television people. She appeared in the glass door with a man of about forty-five with short hair brushed down over his forehead, Czech-intellectual style. He looked familiar, but I couldn't quite place him. They spotted my table and my friend introduced him. "I want you to meet M. He's with Krátký Film." Suddenly it came to me: he was a man I'd spent a whole day fighting to the death. We were in a ghost city in a marble square dotted with fountains. It was terribly, numbingly hot; the sun beat mercilessly on our heads. The only sound in the empty square came from the jets of water in the fountains and the blows of our heavy swords and their echoes as they ricocheted off the palatial façades and monotonous rows of Corinthian columns. I could tell he recognized me too. We gave each other wry smiles, shook each other's limp hands, and mumbled a word or two. How awful these showdowns with ghosts of an un-bridled past! We tried not to let it show, but carrying on a conversation proved a greater torture than battling it out on the sun-scorched marble. Instead of talking directly, we went through our friend, resorting to the most complex devices to avoid addressing each other and to keep our eyes from meeting, but every once in a while I stole a glance at him and behind the lost, purple face caught a glimpse of the hard samurai features silhouetted against the white colonnade. He had worn a pointed gold helmet shaped like a large radish. It shone in the sun, its malevolent luster burning my weary eyes.

The miserable conversation centered on a dachshund cartoon he was working on. The samurai/script writer started rummaging in his briefcase for his script, but because I made him nervous he had trouble finding it and kept pulling out crumpled sheets of paper, piling them on the table with trembling hands that swept them onto the floor. To top it all off, what should fall out of the briefcase but the gold radish helmet, ringing with so pure and provocative a tone that the entire room fell silent and looked over at it, rocking gently before the paralyzed script writer to the tune of "L'important, c'est la rose," which a bloated cavalier with a red waistcoat and a dreamy smile was playing on the piano.

Why is it we constantly drag around with us in our handbags and briefcases the weapons of our nocturnal wars, crystals of solidified poison in boxes lined with scarlet velvet, the head of the Gorgon Medusa, a tongue ripped from a dragon's maw, the mummy of a homunculus, compromising correspondence in Sumerian? Why is it we drag around the terrifying innards of the past, fearing them as we do, smelling the pus they exude, knowing full well that in a bar, a cafe, or a friend's flat Moira the Inexorable will spill them out on the table?

Translated from the Czech by Michael Henry Heim

The Receipt

Karel Čapek

THAT HOT AUGUST EVENING the outdoor cafe on Střelecký Island was crowded, so Minka and Pepa had to seat themselves at a table that was already occupied by a gentleman with a bushy, drooping mustache. "If you don't mind," said Pepa, and the gentleman simply shook his head. (The old nuisance, Minka said to herself, he had to sit right at our table!) So the first thing that happened was that Minka, with the air of a duchess, sat down on the chair which Pepa had wiped off for her with his handkerchief. Next, without further ado, she pulled out her compact and powdered her nose so that even in this heat, God forbid, it wouldn't shine a smidgen. And as she was taking out the compact, a crumpled slip of paper fell from her purse. Immediately the gentleman with the mustache bent down and retrieved it. "You ought to hang on to that, miss," he said gloomily.

Minka turned red, first of all because a strange gentleman had spoken to her, and in the second place because she was annoyed at having turned red. "Thank you," she said, and then she promptly turned back to Pepa. "It's a receipt from the shop where I buy my stockings."

"Precisely," said the melancholy man. "You never know, miss, when it might be needed."

Pepa considered it his duty as a gentleman somehow to intervene. "What do you want to hang on to stupid bits of paper for?" he asked, not looking at the man. "You'd have your pockets stuffed full in no time."

"Makes no difference," the gentleman with the mustache said meaningfully. "Sometimes that's more valuable than I don't know what."

Minka's face acquired a strained expression. (That old nuisance is going to poke his nose right in our conversation; God, why didn't we sit somewhere else!) Pepa decided to put an end to it. "How do you mean, more valuable?" he asked coldly, and he drew his brows together in a frown. (That's so becoming to him, Minka observed admiringly.)

"As a clue," muttered the old nuisance, and in lieu of a formal introduction he added, "What I mean is, I'm Officer Souček, Police Officer Souček, see? We had a case like that just the other day," he said with a wave of his hand. "You never know what you're carrying around in your pockets."

"What sort of case?" Pepa couldn't help asking. (Minka intercepted a glance from a young man at the next table. Just wait, Pepa, I'll fix you for not talking to me!)

"Why, the one about the woman they found way out near Roztyly," said the man with the mustache, and he lapsed into silence.

Minka suddenly picked up interest, no doubt because a woman was involved. "What woman?" she demanded abruptly.

"Why, the one that they found out there," Officer Souček mumbled evasively and, somewhat at a loss, he fished out a cigarette from his pocket. At that point something entirely unexpected happened: Pepa hastily dug his hand into his pocket, produced his lighter, and offered the man a light.

"I thank you," said Officer Souček, obviously touched and honored. "You know, when those harvesters found that dead woman in the cornfield there between Roztyly and Krč," he explained by way of expressing his gratitude and returning the favor.

"I never heard anything about that," said Minka, her eyes widening. "Remember, Pepa, when we were in Krč that time? So what happened to her?"

"Strangled," Officer Souček said matter-of-factly. "She still had the cord around her neck. I won't say anything in front of the young lady here about what she looked like; July, you know, and when she'd already been lying there for something like two months —" With disgust Officer Souček blew out a cloud of smoke. "You wouldn't believe what somebody in that condition looks like. Why, their own mother wouldn't recognize 'em. And the flies —" Officer Souček shook his head mournfully. "Once their skin's gone, miss, it's good-bye and amen to beauty. And it's the devil's own job to identify somebody after that, you know. As long as they've still got eyes and a nose, you can do it; but after lying there more than a month in the sun —"

"But there must have been a monogram somewhere on the corpse," offered Pepa, the expert.

"Forget monograms," grumbled Officer Souček. "Look, single girls don't put their initials on nothing, because they tell themselves, why bother, I'll just be getting married anyway. That female didn't have a single monogram on her, so forget it!"

"And how old was she?" Minka joined in, her interest growing.

"Maybe twenty-five, the doctor said; you know, according to the teeth and so on. And going by her clothes, she looked to be a factory girl or a housemaid, but most likely she was a housemaid, because she had on this kind of petticoat that country girls wear. And besides, if she'd been a factory girl, probably there would've already been a search on for her, because factory girls generally stick to the same job or the same part of town. But when these housemaids switch jobs nobody knows and nobody cares. That's a funny thing about housemaids, but it's true. So we said to ourselves, since it's been two months now and nobody's come looking for her, then she's got to be a housemaid. But the main thing was that receipt."

"What sort of receipt?" Pepa asked eagerly, for he no doubt perceived within himself the heroic makings of a detective, a sea captain, a Canadian trapper or the like, and his face assumed the concentrated and resolute expression required in these situations.

"Well, it was like this," said Officer Souček, gazing mournfully at the ground. "We didn't find nothing on her, nothing. The fellow that did her in took everything that could have been worth something. Except her left hand was still hanging on to a piece of strap from her purse, and the purse minus the strap was found a little farther off in the cornfield. Most likely he was trying to grab her purse, too, but when the strap broke, it wasn't worth nothing anymore, so he threw it out in the field; but he took everything out of it first, you know. So all that was left in it was what had got stuck in the lining, a ticket for the Number Seven streetcar and this receipt from a china shop for a fifty-five-crown purchase. That's all we found."

"But the cord around her neck," said Pepa. "That should've given you something to go on!"

Officer Souček shook his head. "It was only a piece of clothesline, it wasn't any use. We had nothing at all but the streetcar ticket and the receipt. Well, of course we told the newspapers that a female corpse had been found, about twenty-five years of age, gray skirt and striped blouse, and if a housemaid had been missing for about two months, then notify the police at once. We got over a hundred calls; May's the month, you know, when these housemaids usually switch jobs, nobody knows why; but it turned out they were all false alarms. But the amount of work you go to, checking them all out." Officer Souček said gloomily, "You take some little pot-scrubber from a house in Dejvice, say, who turns up again somewhere in Vršovice or Košíře, and you lose a whole day running around. And all for nothing; the silly thing's not only alive and kicking, she's laughing at you. Say, that's a nice tune they're playing now," he remarked, bobbing his head pleasurably to the beat of Wagner's Valkyrie motif, which the cafe band was attacking with all its strength. "Sort of sad, though, isn't it? I'm very partial to sad music. That's why I go to all the big funerals and keep an eye on the pickpockets."

"But the murderer must have left some kind of clue," Pepa supposed.

"See that Casanova-type over there?" asked Officer Souček, suddenly alert. "Ordinarily he goes after collection boxes in churches. I'd like to know what he's up to here. No, the murderer didn't leave any clues. But I can tell you this, when you find a murdered girl, then you can bet her boyfriend did it. That's what usually happens," he said bleakly. "But don't you worry about that, young lady. We would've known who'd done her in, but first we had to find out who she was. That was the hard part, see."

"But surely," Pepa said uncertainly, "the police have their methods."

"Indeed they do," Officer Souček agreed dolefully. "Like the method where you look for a grain of barley in a sack of rice. You need patience, man, patience. You know, I like to read those detective stories, all those microscopes and things.

But why would you look at that poor girl through a microscope? Unless you wanted to see some fat, happy maggot taking his wife and kiddies for a stroll. No offense, miss, but it always vexes me when I hear somebody talk about methods. It's not like reading a book and guessing in advance how it all turns out, you know. It's more like they give you a book and say: All right, Souček, read this word for word, and every time you come across the word 'however,' write down the page number. That's what this job's really like, see. No method's going to help you, and no fancy gimmicks, either. What you have to do is just keep on reading, and at the end you find out there isn't one 'however' in the whole book. Or else you have to run all over Prague and track down the whereabouts of something like a hundred Annas or Markas, until you discover, detective style, that not a one of them's been murdered. That's what somebody ought to write a book about," he said disapprovingly, "and not about the Queen of Sheba's stolen pearl necklace. Because that, friends, is what real detective work is."

"Well, then how did you go about it?" asked Pepa, knowing that he'd have gone about it in a very different way.

"How we went about it," repeated Officer Souček, deep in thought. "First we had to start somewhere, see. Well, to begin with we had that ticket for the Number Seven streetcar. Now just suppose that this girl, if she really was a housemaid, worked in a house somewhere near that streetcar line. That didn't have to be true, maybe she just took that streetcar by chance; but you have to start somewhere, right? Except that Number Seven goes from one end of Prague to the other, from Břevnov by way of Malá Strana and Nové Město to Žižkov; so there wasn't much we could do with that. Then there was that receipt. With that, at least we knew that some time or other she'd bought something from that china shop for fifty-five crowns. So we went to the shop."

"And they remembered her there," Minka burst out.

"Dead wrong, miss," muttered Officer Souček. "They didn't remember her at all. But Dr. Mejzlík, he's our captain, he went there himself and asked what you could buy for fifty-five crowns. 'All kinds of things,' they told him, 'depending on how many things you buy; but for an even fifty-five crowns, there's only this English teapot, just big enough for one.' 'I'll take it then,' our Dr. Mejzlík says, 'but sell it to me wholesale.'

"So then the captain calls me in and says, 'Look, Souček, here's a job for you. Let's assume the girl was a housemaid. Girls like that are always breaking things, but when it happens the third time the mistress of the house tells her, you clumsy goose, this time you pay for it out of your own money. So the girl goes and buys only *one* item, to replace whatever it is she broke. And the only item at fifty-five crowns is this teapot.' 'That's pretty damned expensive,' I says to him. And he says, 'That's the whole point. First of all, it tells us why that housemaid kept the receipt: that was a ton of money for her, and maybe she figured that someday the mistress would pay her back. In the second place, look: this is a teapot for one person only. So either the girl worked for one person only, or else her mistress had a single person for a roomer and the girl was the one who served that person breakfast. And this single person was probably a woman, because a single man would hardly buy himself a nice, expensive teapot like this one; men hardly even notice what they're drinking out of, right? So most likely it was a single woman; because a spinster like that, who's renting a room, always likes something nice that's all her own, and so she buys herself this sort of extravagant, high-priced thing."

"It's true," exclaimed Minka. "You know, Pepa, like that nice little flower vase I have!"

"There you are," said Officer Souček. "But you don't have the receipt. Anyway, then the captain says, 'Now, Souček, let's suppose something else; it's weak as water, but we have to start somewhere. Look, a person who throws fifty-five crowns on a teapot isn't going to live in Žižkov. (Dr. Mejzlík was thinking about that Number Seven line again, that streetcar ticket, you know.) There aren't many roomers in central Prague, and people who live in Malá Strana only drink coffee. I'd guess it would probably be that area where the Number Seven travels between Hradčany and Dejvice. I'd almost say,' he says, 'that a lady who drinks tea from an English teapot like this one could live nowhere but in a little house with a garden. You know the fad these days for anything English, Souček.' You have to understand that sometimes our Dr. Mejzlík gets these wild ideas. 'So what I want you to do, Souček,' he says, 'is take that teapot, go to the part of town where that better class of ladies sublets rooms, and ask questions. And if somebody actually has a teapot just like this one, then find out if a housemaid didn't quit work there sometime in May. It's a damned feeble clue, but we have to give it a shot. So off you go, Souček, it's your case now.'

"Listen, I don't like all this guesswork. A real detective's not some kind of stargazer or fortune-teller. A detective doesn't go in for speculating much; oh, it's true, sometimes you come across the right thing by chance, but chance, that's not what I call honest detective work. That streetcar ticket and that teapot, now at least that's something you can see and get your hands on. But the rest of it's only . . . a figment of the imagination," said Officer Souček, a bit sheepish at having used such an erudite phrase. "So I set about doing it in my own way. I went from house to house in that part of town and asked if they didn't have a teapot like that one around somewhere. And would you believe it, at the forty-seventh house I came to, going right down the line, the housemaid says, 'Oh sure, that's the same kind of teapot this lady who rooms here with the missus has!' So I waited while she went to get the lady of the house. She was a general's widow, see, and she rented out rooms to two ladies. And one of the ladies, a Miss Jakoubková, she was a teacher of English and she had just that kind of teapot for her tea. 'Ma'am,' I says, 'didn't you have a maid who left here sometime in May?' 'That's right,' says the landlady, 'we called her Mařka, but what her other name was, I don't remember.' 'And sometime before that, didn't this girl break a teapot?' 'She did,' says the landlady, 'and she had to buy a new one out of her own pocket. But my goodness, how did you know about that?' 'Well, ma'am,' says I, 'we hear just about everything.'

"So after that it was easy; first of all I found out who the housemaid was that this Mařka was best friends with — housemaids always have a girlfriend, just one, but she tells her everything — and from her I found that the girl's name was Mařka Pařížková and she came from Dřevice. But most of all I wanted to know who the young man was this Mařka went out with. The friend said she thought it was somebody named Franta. Who this Franta was, she didn't know, but she remembered that she went with the two of them to the Eden Dance Hall once, and that some young Casanova there had called out to this Franta, 'Hey, Ferda!' Well, then we referred the case to Officer Fryba in our division; he's the expert on these aliases, you know. And right away Fryba says, 'Franta alias Ferda, that would be this fellow from Košíře who calls himself Kroutil, but his real name is Pastýřík. Captain, sir, I'll go get him, but there needs to be two of us to do it.' So I went with him myself, although that's not really my line of work. We collared this Pastýřík at his girlfriend's; it was pretty nasty, he wanted to shoot it out. Then Captain Matička went to work on him back at the station. Nobody knows how he does it, but in sixteen hours' time he got everything out of Pastýřík, how he did in this Mařka Pařížková in the cornfield right after she got off work and then robbed her of a few crowns. Of course, he'd promised to marry her — they all do that," Officer Souček added gloomily.

Minka shuddered. "Pepa," she breathed, "that's awful!"

"Not now it isn't," Officer Souček said solemnly. "What was awful was when we were standing there by her body in that field and all we could find was that receipt and that streetcar ticket. Two tiny, good-for-nothing bits of paper — but all the same, we evened the score for poor Mařka. Like I told you, never throw nothing away, nothing. Even the least little thing can turn out to be a clue or a piece of evidence. No sir, you never know what's in your pocket that might be important."

Minka sat perfectly still, her eyes filled with tears. And suddenly, with a warm burst of affection, she turned to her Pepa and from her moist hand let fall to the ground the crumpled receipt which, the entire time, she had been nervously pressing between her fingers. Pepa didn't see it, because he was gazing up at the stars. But Officer Souček saw it and, sadly and knowingly, he smiled.

Translated from the Czech by Norma Comrada

Mendelssohn Is on the Roof

Jiří Weil

TO BE MASTER of a conquered land on its way to becoming a German land is tiring and enervating work. Life was better in those long-ago days before they seized power, when he could fight the enemies of the Reich directly, when he could chase them around the room at meetings and then connect with a fist to the jaw. Life was better when he could see the enemy standing before him, visible, blood trickling down his face, and he could stomp on him with his high boots, polished until they veritably glistened. Life was better at Columbus-Haus, where he could interrogate conspirators of the Night of the Long Knives, watching the blood soak through the plaster walls of his office. Life was better in the Polish campaign, dropping bombs on villages from his own plane and then, because the Poles had no anti-aircraft guns, flying low, barely above the ground, in order to see the cottages burning, the confused human vermin racing back and forth, the dead bodies lying on the ground, frying in the flames.

He had fought the enemy face to face in those days. Now he only gives orders to bring about its destruction. He is master of hundreds and thousands of subjects, setting a complex machinery into action, making sure it operates well, checking its various parts, improving them, perfecting them,

Chapter eight of *Mendelssohn Is on the Roof.*

introducing technological innovations, all the while remaining invisible himself, receiving figures, reports, and graphs, signing death sentences without ever seeing the condemned, going in to check the results only on occasion.

But to be master of the land is the task assigned him by the Leader. It means that he must renounce everything personal, that he must be alone, that he must have no friends, that he must be inscrutable and inaccessible even at home among his family, even at parties and dinners. All that remains for him is music; it always helps when he feels tired; it offers peace and contentment; the tensions of the day melt away in it. He remembers listening to Beethoven's Fourth after the Night of the Long Knives, remembers how it gave him renewed strength to carry on, to continue interrogating enemies and beating confessions out of them. The music cleansed everything that time, even the blood.

But now he can no longer listen as he pleases. Though he has an excellent phonograph in Panenské Břežany, one that is not for sale anywhere but was a personal gift from the director of Siemens, and though he has records of virtually the entire classical repertory, still he rarely plays them, because he doesn't like canned music, however well produced. He no longer plays in the amateur quartet — his playing has gotten too rusty and his hand can no longer hold a bow, because he has used it too often on police duty.

What about concerts and opera performances? Nowadays these bring him little pleasure. They're official occasions organized to honor some important event or visitor; mainly they serve as background for official gatherings. Even the house concerts of chamber music at the Waldstein Palace aren't actually "house" concerts but social evenings to which he is obliged to invite all sorts of people — generals, big shots of the SS Elite Guard, the highest officers of the Gestapo, chance visitors. These people have no interest in classical music — they would prefer operettas or films with Marika Rokk. They attend these concerts because they don't know how to get out of it tactfully, while he, on the other hand, has to invite them to discharge obligations.

Small wonder, then, that they're bored, that they yawn, inspect their fingernails, cough and clear their throats, clean their monocles, and even doze off. How can he possibly enjoy music under such circumstances? What good is it to invite the finest musicians and conductors of the Reich to Prague, when they must perform for such uneducated audiences, who applaud only dutifully and never with enthusiasm. And, of course, the artists sense this immediately; they have a well-developed instinct about their audiences. Therefore, they play and sing any old way, without distinction, and instead of demonstrating the strength of their artistry, they spend their entire day running around the city shopping for goods and foodstuffs. They demand special rations allowing them to bring home bacon, poultry, and woolens.

Even tonight he is expected to attend an opera perform-ance — Mozart again, *Don Giovanni,* at the Stavovský Thea-ter. The opera had its first performance there and it would be performed there again today, the day the stolen theater is to be restored to German hands. What better opera to invite the minister of the Reich, the Leader's favorite, to attend? He had escorted the distinguished guest around for the whole day before entrusting him to the head of the Central Bureau, who was to show him the Jewish memorials. The Acting Reich Protector's kindness did not go so far as to actually showing him Jews. Besides, the head of the Central Bureau was better suited to it — he himself knows nothing and wants to know nothing about the Jews besides the Leader's command — that they be annihilated. This command would be carried out, but it was easier to do so if one saw the Jews only as numbers instead of having to actually meet them in real life.

They rode along the quay together. He had the roof of the car down so they could better inspect the city. They looked at the river and at the royal castle. The view was most beautiful from there. The quay had been completed a hundred years earlier, when Prague was a German city. He sat beside the minister and spoke to him about the monuments, about musicians and composers who had visited Prague. The minister knew a great deal about the city — he had undoubtedly studied a number of illustrated books back in Berlin. It was strange to discover that this former architect, well known for his grandiose plans for the reconstruction of Berlin and for the construction of an art center in Linz, took such pleasure in this city. Surely it must seem small and provincial to him compared to Berlin or Vienna. The minister said, "Music in stone," and truly this phrase, bandied about by authors of art books, described Prague well. The city was, indeed, steeped in music and brought into harmony by it. The guest wanted to see the German House of Art and expressed a desire to visit the opera. Fortunately, they were playing *Don Giovanni* at the Stavovský Theater. It would be a good performance and something to boast about.

They continued across the Charles Bridge to the castle. He particularly singled out the statue of Roland as incontrovertible evidence that Prague had always been German. The

guest admired the statue on artistic grounds but didn't seem
to get the symbolic significance, nor did he take any notice of
the sword the statue was clutching in its hand. He was more
interested in the statue's face. But of course the former architect was one of the few intellectuals in the Leader's inner
circle. He had never been a soldier, he didn't wear a uniform,
and he had come to Prague in a civilian coat and hat.

Slowly they drove uphill toward the castle through the old
neighborhood called Malá Strana — and the minister asked
to have the car stopped every so often in order to admire the
palaces' facades.

"It most certainly is a German city," the minister thought
out loud, "erected by German builders, but . . ."

"There are no buts," his host interrupted him sharply. "The
Czechs always lived here as temporary guests. It's German to
the core."

"Yes, you're right, you're certainly right. The Leader, after
all, said the same thing when he returned from Prague. Its
architecture seemed more German to him than the architecture of Vienna. But . . . the German builders hired Czech
artisans. We architects have a trained eye, we can see that they
brought a foreign element into their work. They worked in
their own fashion. When you picture Nürnberg . . ."

"But Prague is baroque," his host interrupted him a bit
peevishly.

"Of course, but after all, the Prague baroque is different
from the baroque in other cities — Munich, for instance, or
Dresden."

They drove up to the castle and walked about the courtyards.

"What sort of army is this?" asked the minister when he

saw the castle guard. "I've never seen uniforms like these with canary-yellow lapels."

"That's the Czech national guard — a real joke. The state President lives in one wing here."

"I hope we don't have to visit him."

"No, he comes to visit me. Or rather, he doesn't come, but Frank brings him. That flag is also just for show. We had to leave them something."

They stopped by the Cathedral of St. Vitus.

"The Czechs have always had a megalomanic streak. Wouldn't you like to go inside? They have the vaults of Czech kings there, and the crown jewels as well. I have the keys to the crown jewels, but, of course, I don't carry them with me." He smiled. "Shall we go in?"

"I'm afraid we have little time," said the minister, "and I've kept you from your official duties long enough."

"Not at all," he protested. "I'm very honored to be able to acquaint you with the beauties of Prague." In fact, he was glad he didn't have to enter the cathedral.

He had unpleasant memories of the cathedral. The state President, though he barely reached Heydrich's shoulder, had hunched even lower as he handed him the keys to the crown jewels and humbly thanked him for returning three of them. He was repulsed to see the old man kiss the death's-head of St. Václav, as if hoping St. Václav would have mercy on his land.

On the other hand, he was happy to point out the statue of St. George to the minister. The Leader had admired it enormously after arriving at the head of his armies to take possession of the conquered land for Germany. It seemed to symbolize the Reich itself. Snakes and lizards slither at its base, and a ferocious dragon rears its head out of the mud, dirt, and mire. The hero in armor stabs the dragon with his pennanted lance. That's how the Reich triumphs over its enemies! The Leader had first thought of moving the statue to the Reich Chancellery, but after looking it over again carefully he changed his mind. His unfailing artistic and political instinct warned him of something. He called in a professor of art history from the German University, an expert on Prague, and confirmed that his instinct was right. The statue had originally been German; indeed, commissioned by Charles, Emperor of the Holy Roman Empire. It was a Gothic statue. But then in the sixteenth century it had been recast by some Czech bungler. That's why it didn't have the proper German proportions. The hero was smaller than the horse and his face didn't have the properly severe, constricted, emaciated look of a German hero. He looked like a regular Czech pancake of a fellow. Thus the corrupted statue could not be an embellishment of the German Chancellery but remained in the castle courtyard.

"I'll show you the spot where the Leader looked out over Prague. It was actually from a second-floor window, but the view is the same."

They were silent for a few moments as they looked at the view.

"The German students rightly named Prague 'The Golden City.' Fortunately, Göring didn't have it bombed. Otherwise we'd see only ruins today."

"I've seen enough of them in Berlin," complained the minister bitterly.

Heydrich frowned. He disliked hearing about the bombing of German cities.

The minister continued, "We'll build a new Berlin after the war, a Berlin with broad, airy streets and parks, with grand squares and modern buildings. The conquered nations will pay for it, so we won't have to count pennies. But this city will probably remain a museum."

"Yes, a museum." Heydrich suddenly remembered. "The head of the Central Bureau is waiting for you in the Černinský Palace. My chauffeur will take you there. I must leave you now, but I'll see you tonight at the opera."

The minister sat back again in the car. He was annoyed with himself for getting into a dangerous conversation with Heydrich. One had to be very careful with these military types. He had noticed Heydrich's reaction when he had mentioned the bombing of Berlin.

The head of the Central Bureau courteously opened the door of his car for the minister. They drove back down to the city.

"You're about to see an entirely different neighborhood, the former Jewish ghetto. Otherwise, we'd keep the Jews there temporarily as they do in Warsaw. But there are interesting historical sights: the old Jewish cemetery, the Jewish Town Hall with the clock that runs backward, and then our great secret, a Jewish museum."

The head of the Central Bureau was certainly better company than Heydrich. He obviously didn't stand on military ceremony, nor was he a stone-face like Heydrich, before whom one had to watch one's every word. And the tour of the exhibits really intrigued him. Even the blowing of that curious horn in the gloomy halflight of the museum amused him. They said their good-byes at the hotel near the main railroad station. He needed to rest a bit, take a bath, and change clothing before going to the theater. . . .

"I'll be at the theater, too," said the head of the Central Bureau. "May I have the honor of visiting you during the intermission?"

The Stavovský Theater was especially illuminated in honor of the Reich minister's visit. In the presidential box he was greeted by Heydrich, who presented his wife to him, and then the wife of the Secretary of State, Frank, and finally the Secretary of State himself. Heydrich offered the minister a seat next to his wife. Standing behind them, at respectful attention, were his adjutants. The minister stood out in his evening clothes: looking out over the audience, he saw only men in uniforms and women in formal attire. This preponderance of tassels, cuffs, and epaulets seemed inappropriate for such a lovely and delicate theater, with its gilded rococo ornamentation in which angels were the predominant motif. Chubby angels and bemedaled military types in high boots that squeaked at the smallest movement of the feet — these did not go together. Actually Mozart himself was not suited to people in uniform. But the audience listened quietly and attentively once the music began. Perhaps the music was so strong that it penetrated even brains dulled by murder and alcohol. Perhaps they forgot about their bloody trade — at least for a while. It was also pleasant not to have this outstanding performance disturbed by the screaming of sirens.

During the intermission Heydrich's wife started a conversation with him. She questioned him about Berlin as if she were longing to return to the main city of the Reich. She tried to give the impression of being in exile among barbarians here, but her rounded, well-nourished figure suggested that life in the Protectorate suited her well. This time he was careful not to say a word about bombing. He talked about the inner workings of the Reich Chancellery, about the Leader's cabinet, about receptions organized by Göring in the Karinhalle . . . and, of course, about Prague. He had come to appreciate its beauties, thanks to his most competent guide. Even Frank joined the discussion about Prague, describing what the city had looked like during the Republic, when he'd fought against the thieving Czech parliament.

"They stole this theater from us. They took a theater dedicated to German art and they degraded it with perverse French drawing-room comedies and yokelish hodgepodges by Czech authors."

It was clear that hatred and spite were pouring out of Frank, that his words did not reflect the feelings of a ruler and master of the land such as Heydrich, but rather those of a person who had finally quenched his desire for revenge.

The adjutants brought refreshments — French wine for the gentlemen and real orangeade for the ladies. They chatted easily in the comfortable box, everyone smiling. Only Heydrich stood to the side, his face expressionless.

When the head of the Central Bureau suddenly appeared, young and full of good spirits as if exhilarated by the music, Heydrich interrupted the conversation in a commanding voice, without any regard for his guest, "I haven't had a chance to read your report. Is Terezín in full swing? Have all the Czech inhabitants been moved out?"

"Yes," announced the head of the Central Bureau. "The order has been carried out, the Czech inhabitants moved, and transports dispatched regularly. Some of them stop just briefly and then continue immediately to the East. The construction of a special Terezín/Bohušovice line is being considered, to facilitate the operation. But the Jews would have to put it up themselves!"

"Good," said Heydrich, and then he thought of another thing. "Giesse" — he turned around — "has the statue of that Jew, Mendelssohn, on the balustrade been torn down? You seem to have forgotten to inform me about it."

"I haven't had a chance to do so, sir, but everything is in order. The statue was torn down this afternoon."

Heydrich fell silent again. But the mood was spoiled.

Heydrich's wife complained to the minister, "You men can't stay away from business even in the theater! And the Jews, on top of everything! Really, people shouldn't speak of them in polite society." The rebuke was aimed at the head of the Central Bureau.

"You can be sure, Madame, that in the very near future there will be absolutely no need to talk about Jews in any sort of society." The head of the Central Bureau smiled and stepped away so that the minister could resume his interrupted conversation.

The head of the Central Bureau looked around the hall, which was beginning to fill up again. The gold of uniforms and women's precious jewels glistened everywhere. Some faces were joyfully agitated by the music, others were calm and cheerful. As if there weren't a war going on at all, as if they had all met here to celebrate a victory, as if they put on their dress uniforms and ordered their wives to wear their most expensive jewelry. How strange it all was . . . and at that moment he thought of his most recent trip to the East. He had just returned from there two days ago and now, as he stood in the box decorated with the sovereign emblem of the Reich, it seemed a different world.

A desolate countryside in the rain, a black, barren plain shrouded with smoke and fog, the loading platform of the railroad station, the cattle cars out of which staggered the half-suffocated people with stars — men, women, and children with bundles and suitcases. And the SS policemen beating them with clubs, hurrying them along, pushing them into the thick mud and then stamping on them with their heavy studded boots. Cries and blood, screaming children, blows and pistols, the long road to the camp and the dead bodies lying along the roadside. And the smoke from the chimneys pouring out day and night, fog and mud, barbed wire and high towers with machine guns. Dirt and blood, the hiss of gas in tiled chambers that resembled bathrooms, ashes covering the earth, fields of the thousands cremated.

He smiled contentedly. They all pretend they know nothing. They don't want to know anything. They can't even bear to hear a word about the Jews. He is happy that he knows what is going on in the East. Heydrich, of course, knows too, but he never lets on that he is pleased with the good work of his subordinates.

The orchestra was beginning to tune up. It was time to say their good-byes, above all to the distinguished guest who was returning to Berlin that very night. A little later the sweet music of Mozart rang out through the theater once again.

Translated from the Czech by Marie Winn

A Prague Eclogue

Jiří Kovtun

L U D V Í K   L A Y beneath the broad crown of a beech tree in a Prague park and felt pretty good even though the war was still going on around him. It was a Saturday afternoon, May 5, 1945. Lacking a slender flute to play on, Ludvík puckered his lips and whistled a tune to pass the time. He was eighteen years old, dressed in civilian clothes, and waiting for his friend Kamil, who was also eighteen, and also a civilian.

Someone was approaching Ludvík, but it wasn't Kamil. It was a man, well over thirty and wearing the olive green uniform of a German soldier. He came walking along the wide, straight path strewn with a layer of yellow sand. At first his footsteps were inaudible, but the nearer he came, the louder became the irregular crunch of the gravel, for the footfalls came in fits and starts, as though beyond the walker's control. From time to time he looked around him, and as he drew nearer, Ludvík realized the soldier had company. Something small and excitable ran out of the bushes and rolled along the path like a ball. Then Ludvík heard a wheezy bark. It was a poodle, which ran up to the soldier and put its two forepaws on the soldier's knees, waiting for a pat. The soldier smiled and while he bent over he looked in Ludvík's direction to share the smile, half for the poodle, which in the meantime had bounded away again, and half for Ludvík, who had no interest in it.

Part I of *A Prague Eclogue.*

Ludvík was sure the soldier would come over to him, offer
him a reassuring smile, and say something. He decided to
ignore him. Then again, he thought, this might be the wrong
thing to do. Perhaps he ought to try to explain everything to
the soldier despite his bad German. But wouldn't that be a
mistake? How could he ever explain anything to a German?
Still, it might not be a bad idea if someone were to let the
soldier know exactly where he was before it all came to an
end. At the far end of an imaginary line joining Ludvík and
the soldier, the sharp outline of the high summer palace walls
could be seen through a transparent curtain of sparse birch
trees: the summer palace was part of it too. He decided to
spell it out for the soldier but since he wasn't worth the bother
Ludvík would not say it out loud. So he began telling the
soldier a story, in his mind:

Listen, then. Once upon a time there was a king.
A king, did I say? That's an exaggeration. Actually, he
was a vice-regent in the kingdom of Bohemia, and his
name was Ferdinand. And there was this girl called
Philippina. We'll come to that in a moment. Perhaps
Ferdinand had a ruddy complexion, well-stuffed with
rich, fatty fare (out on his horse every day before dawn
— still picking his teeth — to hunt snipe in the
marshes), or he could have had pale, sunken cheeks
(vigils, religious discipline, hours of eschatological
meditation), and it's possible he had a beard, though
maybe he didn't, I couldn't say. Hands he certainly did
have, and with those hands he drew an outline, a six-
pointed star. It was a plan. This is where my wife shall
live. I'll come and visit her. Every day I shall ride west-

wards from Prague Castle, through the deep valley, and
stay the night. Hvězda — the Star Summer Palace. We
live in times when astronomy has discarded the garments of superstition and parades in the classical na-
kedness of science. Smooth walls, my love, austere
forms, a regular pattern. But within, it was warm —
murals, paintings, candelabra, light. The plans were
ready, the Spanish and German master builders had approved, and soon the timber skeleton was being clothed
in the flesh of walls. Philippina Welser — now we're
getting to it — Philippina Welser, the secretly (but law-
fully) wedded wife of the vice-regent Ferdinand moved
into the furnished chambers. She moved in so quickly
that if she looked out the window she might have seen
a forgotten mason's trowel still lying in the grass. There
were painted ceilings above her head, crystal vases on
her tables, tapestries on her walls; there was milk and
honey for her breakfast, venison for her lunch. And
now, a discreet sideways glance beyond the walls of the
game-park into the nearby village, where a poor family
lived on dry bread while waiting for their skinny hen to
lay an egg. But never mind. Whenever Philippina came
out onto the green pasture in front of the palace, the
startled peacocks would scatter; whenever she crossed
the meadow on the northern slope she would catch the
smell of horses from the stables almost hidden in the
valley. Every day huntsmen would come for their orders
and then vanish into the deep woods, returning later
with their soft, warm, bleeding catch. The arrival of her
lover — I mean her husband — was always heralded by
a procession of musicians and cooks coming to prepare

a boisterous celebration. Many of the guests would get up in the middle of the feast and slip away to a small, foul-smelling chamber to tickle their gullet with a feather until they retched and vomited up all they had eaten, before returning to the banquet and filling their emptied stomachs once more. It makes me feel sick, but that's how it was.

But bad times were on their way. Before then, though, the Emperor Rudolf with his entourage of sages, charlatans, mountebanks, and mistresses would make occasional visits to the Star Palace, where revelry and learned discussion would help him pass the time remaining to him between reason and madness. And I'd be very surprised if the word "star" didn't conjure up for him the unmentionable idea of the unknown metal, the ellipse, the imaginary line etched in darkness. Once, when he had retired to his mistress's chamber in the south-southwestern point of the Star Palace and was about to snuff out the last candle, he discovered that he was still holding a glass retort. I made that bit up, but it could easily have happened. I expect you've been to the Golden Lane at the Prague Castle, where the emperor's chemists searched for the philosopher's stone, and year after year the alchemists boiled water in closed flasks. No doubt you said *schön* or *dröllig*, but what do you know about this city and its experiments? Not a thing.

And then it happened. Fate decreed that a legend be created for teachers to lecture about in hallowed tones and arouse a gentle twitch in our mothers' eyes whenever it was mentioned. I refer to Bílá Hora — the battle of White Mountain. What does it mean to you? Some

important sentence ("The fate of Europe was decided
for several centuries hence") that has survived the
moldering of textbooks in the attic and stuck in your
memory? Twenty-seven thousand against twenty-one
thousand, two hours of battle just after midday. A beautiful scene from a bird's-eye view (well, they still fought
in bright colors in those days, like football teams, the
greens versus the yellows, the blues versus the reds). It
ended at the wall behind you. This is how I imagine it:
A calm as terrible as the din of battle, the silence of the
dead whose cries had slipped away like fish in a stream,
the silence of the slain with swords protruding from
their lungs. When all the others had taken to their
heels, the Moravians fought to the last man with their
backs to that wall. This contrasts with the following
scene: In the palace kitchens hot steam rises from
bleeding turkey-cocks that lie in a long row, on the wide
table all ready for the victors' banquet. . . . But the murder and mayhem would last thirty years. We didn't invite them in, but they came and went as if they were at
home, all those Bavarians, Swabians, Brandenburgers,
Danes, Swedes, Croatians, Frenchmen, Saxons, Switz-
ers, and Spaniards. They marched through our land and
left death in their wake, death and a bit of new life:
dumb amazement and bastard embryos (all too often
women's laps were mistaken for a field of battle). By the
time the bones of those who had fallen in the early years
had bleached white, history lazily turned full circle and
things went back to the way they were at the beginning.
Fortunately there were countless violated virgins and
hoards of cripples, innumerable graves, and scorched

earth, not to mention gibbet-covered hilltops and rivers on which ice formed red in the winter, or it wouldn't have been obvious what history had meant by taking that meander. There had been worse battles when you think of it; only a handful perished on this wood-flanked plain. But this is where it all began.

I say this is where it all began. When, as children, we wandered through the dry fields and discovered crumbly lumps of chalk (hopscotch on the asphalt, a game called "Heaven, Hell, Paradise"), little did we know that we were walking on the spot from which the souls of dying soldiers had winged upwards (Heaven), until one day on a sorrowful walk my father, with a grim expression on his face, told me the whole truth (Hell), and my mother tempered the bitterness his thoughts had induced with her gentle, female languor (Paradise). It remains in my memory like a message from earlier generations. I have it from poetry and the reproachful articles in the pre-Protectorate schoolbooks: "for three centuries we groaned." For a long time I took it literally. But it's wrong. Actually, for three centuries we were silent. And that wasn't necessarily such a bad thing.

How can I explain? You see, it's no great misfortune to be erased from history for a while, to rest and sleep and not to take part for centuries in all the heart-searching and mental anguish that sap the strength of nations as surely as constant carousing will. It's rejuvenation therapy. While you Germans were growing older, time here stood still. At a time when your Kant was falling prey to hypochondria and breathing only through his nose for fear of catching a cold, while he was weaving his

complex ideas on those monotonous walks of his, and
your Goethe was experimenting in art with every possible form, color, and taste, our thoughts and speech
were on the level of children. All we had left were nurs-
ery rhymes, songs, and simple tunes inspired by the
babbling of brooks. Then Monsieur Rousseau, who
confessed to so much about himself, walked through
unspoiled landscapes and discovered the sentimental
barbarian. We were here and had almost everything.
We quickly tried to make up for lost time through fresh
thinking, and the candle that Lazarus was carrying
when he left the sepulchre shone into the farthest
corners of those centuries. We found our old selves
again on the cliff-tops, in the ruins of castles, in the
cathedral tower. But it doesn't matter where we found
ourselves, the main thing is that we did. . . .

"*Guten Tag,*" said the soldier, and looked at Ludvík lying
beneath the broad crown of the beech tree and feeling pretty
good even though the war was still going on around him.

They were in the Star game-park, which lies to the west of
the city and stretches south from the Summer Palace, within
the limits of Greater Prague. You enter the park through the
main gate on the eastern side. Nearby there used to be two
pubs, now almost abandoned at the end of the war, but fre-
quented before the war by hungry and thirsty day-trippers.
On summer Sundays men with their sleeves rolled up and
women with their hair hanging loose would sit outside at the
round tables listening to off-color jokes cracked by the emcee
as he introduced a schmaltzy band. The children would
impatiently rumple the tablecloths and strike up lightning

friendships or longingly follow the tubby nougat vendor with their eyes as he threaded his way among the tables. A sign hung at the park gate with commandments for nature lovers (DON'T LEAVE LITTER — USE THE LITTER BINS — TOILETS, 100 YARDS ON THE RIGHT) plus a timetable of opening and closing times for different seasons of the year. But during the final years of the war, someone made a hole in the park wall that allowed access at all times. Courting couples staying overtime no longer had to fear being locked in.

Ludvík and his two friends, Kamil and Artur, used to enter the park either through the main gate or through the new hole in the wall, depending on their mood and where they happened to be at the time. Usually they would arrive together, but on those occasions when, for some reason or other, they failed to meet on the streets of Břevnov, they would meet in the park itself. The grammar school in the city center, which all three attended and where they were all in the same class, had been closed since the beginning of the year. Once a week they would meet with the teachers who had been forced to work in factories and written assignments would be collected and given out. But even so, such emergency schooling was only available to some. Most of the students had been dispatched by the Protectorate authorities to the Moravian frontier zone to build the last fortifications and trenches of this war, or to take part in other useful war work.

Ludvík, Kamil, and Artur were not regarded as useful to the war effort. In February they were split up for a time. Ludvík had stayed in Prague. He was exempted from forced labor by a medical certificate stating that he had a heart condition; he had obtained the certificate on some earlier occasion to get out of gym at school (too lazy to take part). Kamil had gone off on fortification work to Moravská Ostrava and

Artur had convinced the authorities that staying with relatives in the country could be considered essential war work by having it classified as agricultural labor.

At the end of April, by which time it was clear that the war could be over any day, the three of them met again in Prague. Artur, loath to abandon his South Bohemian village where he had felt free, was lured back by a letter from Ludvík telling him that something was brewing in Prague that he shouldn't miss out on. In his German village in Silesia, Kamil had still not been issued a spade when he was sent back to Prague. The three of them lived close to each other in Břevnov. Their windows all looked out on the same view: the Benedictine monastery on the slope across the valley, where the westbound road leaves Prague via White Mountain. On Saturday, May 5, only Ludvík and Kamil had planned to meet; Artur, whose romantic nature was a family mystery, had been kept in until after lunch to do the chores.

Ludvík arrived at the rendezvous under the broad beech tree half an hour early and had enough time to think things over. Above all, he thought about how the war was actually coming to an end, and how history was reaching a visible turning point, and he was there to see it. On his way to the park, the streets of Břevnov had been livelier than he had ever known them. People were walking about with buckets of whitewash, laughing and joking. Some were drunk, others reeled in delight at the long-forgotten taste of freedom. They called out to neighbors and saluted the tricolor Czechoslovak flags. Their numbers were growing all the time. As they walked through the streets, the world before their eyes was already different from the one behind them, for they were the living dividing line. In front of them, there were still signs in Czech and German; behind them were only the sounds of their mother tongue (someone had actually shouted out: long live our beautiful Czech language!). Audaciously, people did exactly what they felt like doing, though the advancing allied armies were still a long way off and German soldiers, bewildered and apathetic, were roaming the city in confusion. Ludvík himself had been momentarily caught up in the throng. In front of the butcher's shop, he had supported a young girl on his shoulder as she painted out the sign METZGEREI to the laughter and applause of the crowd, while Ludvík felt the pressure of two hard knees on his neck. After he had left the crowd by the old school and turned into Zeyer Avenue, which slopes up between the fields toward the park, he could still hear the singing behind him.

Then he thought about Kamil and his parents. Last Monday, two uniformed policemen, one German and one Czech, had come asking for Kamil's father. When they learned he was not at home, they went away without stating their business and they had not been back again. Kamil had told Ludvík to have no fears for his father: he was with relatives somewhere, but Kamil had been unwilling to go into detail. Ludvík hoped for Kamil's sake that everything would turn out all right and that he would see his father again soon. That everything would turn out all right was the one thing he was sure of.

"*Guten Tag,*" the soldier said.

Go to hell, thought Ludvík. But what could he do? He replied, "*Guten Tag.*"

The soldier called the poodle to him after it had gone back and forth several times between them and cautiously touched Ludvík's leg with its nose. Then Ludvík heard, "*Sie haben's gut.* It's peaceful here, isn't it? Chaos everywhere, everything happening at once, but here it's peaceful. You have it good."

Ludvík said, "*Ich verstehe nicht.*"

It was not entirely true that he did not understand. He understood most of the words and their entire meaning, even though the soldier spoke with a regional accent.

"*Gut. Gut hier,*" the soldier said, drawing such a wide circle with his arm that he ended up turning his back on Ludvík. It was an enormous gesture that encompassed the entire wood and the scenes of destruction in foreign parts. Ludvík could not deny that he understood.

"*Ich verstehe, gut,*" he said.

"*Ja,* we're going away soon," said the soldier pointing to himself.

Only now did Ludvík look the soldier in the face. He saw the features of a man about forty years old. He found him neither attractive nor repulsive. The face neither concealed nor revealed very much.

"*Ja,*" said Ludvík.

"We'll be marching off soon," said the soldier, and looked at his dog. Ludvík thought to himself: What will happen to the dog when they leave? This is no war for dogs. (A dog offensive, dogs with white flags, dogs in a P.O.W. camp.) Maybe the soldier was thinking the same thing. No, this was no war for dogs.

"*Komisch, nicht wahr, dieser Hund?*"

"*Ja,* it's a funny dog, all right."

"Actually it's a bitch. She's just had babies. *Zwillinge.*"

"*Bitte?*"

"Twins." The soldier pronounced the last word through two upraised fingers of his right hand. Again, Ludvík could not pretend not to understand.

"*Ach, ja,*" he said, and everything began to seem absurd. It was absurd that today, possibly just a few hours before the end of the war, a German soldier was here, strolling through the woods, as if the defeated army had nothing better to do. And it was absurd that the unknown foreigner was about to make him a portentous offer, which would be refused and would fail to bridge the two worlds. He knew what was coming.

The poodle darted off among the low-hanging branches of the trees and for a moment was lost to their gaze. The soldier, as if the dog were a third person whose absence gave them the opportunity for a quick exchange of confidences, pointed into the green thicket where they could hear the dog's breathy panting, then leaned toward Ludvík and said, "You can have the dog if you want. I have no more use for it."

No, not on your life, Ludvík said to himself. That's all I need. A poodle. A hippopotamus. An elephant. Mist. Mephisto. That's not a dog's shape. What do I need a ghost in the house for? That's an old trick. No thanks. Keep it and go away.

"*Nein*," said Ludvík, and the soldier did not insist.

Then Ludvík noticed that the soldier had a limp (when, after repeated whistling, the poodle failed to reappear from the undergrowth, the soldier walked with an unsteady gait to the other side of the path to call it back) and the thought that there were still soldiers who went for strolls at a time like this did not seem so absurd any more. He followed his uneven steps (an iambic foot: accented vowel, unaccented vowel) and caught himself feeling first sympathy, then shame for his sympathy. Finally he realized that sympathy was nothing to be ashamed of and anyway nobody knew about it. From all indications, the soldier must have been billeted in the new school that had been turned into a military hospital at the very beginning of the war. Education continued there in a different form. Everyone brought there had a new learning experience. They learned the alphabet of pain: A for amputation, B for bandage, C for cystoscope.

The soldier was standing in front of him with the poodle in his arms.

"*Schöne Stadt, Prag.*"

"*Ja*, it's beautiful."

"*Und glücklich.* Lucky, too. Other cities: bombing raids, ruins, but not here in Prague. Dresden, terrible, my sister wrote me about it. But Prague, almost untouched."

The soldier used only basic expressions so that Ludvík should understand him. Ludvík understood, but each had something different on his mind.

The river first flows through this city (thought the soldier) and then through others. Here unbroken bridges, banks of blossom, and tall buildings are reflected in the water, but farther on, the reflections are of ruins, conflagration, scorched banks, a city with its belly ripped open and its innards hanging out. I'm writing to you from the dead city of Dresden, he had read in his sister's letter. The planes dropped incendiary bombs and everything was set on fire — the houses, the trees, the grass, the earth, and even the water. People fleeing their houses like living torches and leaping into the emergency water tanks that dotted the city, but often it was only a choice between burning to death or drowning. Then other bombers arrived and flattened the burning city. Street after street disappeared in ruins, as if the city had been plowed under by a giant plow. They all died indiscriminately: the young, the old, the ugly, the beautiful, the bad, the good, women, men, babes in arms, babies about to leave the womb, old people who would have died the next day from old age, invalids, the blind, the deaf and dumb, the feebleminded, schoolchildren, thieves, soldiers, SS men, fugitives, horses, dogs, cats, canaries. A huge pile of corpses was heaped up on the main square, which now resembled an enormous crater, thousands of bodies whose skulls, innards, and limbs were all mixed up together. Then an enormous fire was made of the pile. The same river. Two different cities.

Of course it's a beautiful city (thought Ludvík), but you don't understand why. This city lies in a lovely hollow in the midst of a country buzzing with bees, where flocks of birds sing, where there are as many beasts in the forest as grains of sand in the sea or stars in the sky, where there are so many cattle that the pastures can scarcely feed them and their herds outnumber the hoards of grasshoppers in the meadows. In this land the waters are clean and tasty fish swim in them. And this city lies in a valley beneath a high hill that coils like a dolphin, the pig of the sea. That's the way it is, and you know nothing about it. And you don't know either that all the adventures I've had in this city started in the suburbs with the first smells of my childhood (hot asphalt, chamomile, a fresh bread-roll during recess at school, vegetables and Mediterranean fruit in crates outside the shops). Every new foray deeper into the city brought fresh discoveries, but for a long time I used to look at this city through a few cracks in the suburbs, which were a world all to themselves. My first vista: a tram ride to the Sborowitz department store to buy a new sailor suit, the bitter mothball smell of the textile department, the elevator operators, the glass-roofed halls bathed in sunlight. My second vista: a visit to the market with the smell of butter, cheese, fish, and a new smell — never to be obliterated by the smoke of later adventures — the scent of newly printed broadsheets with fairy tales on them that a smiling Slovak woman gave me at one of the stalls. And then the vistas broadened and the smells became mixed, but I never stopped looking at the city from the vantage point of the periphery and my childhood. But that's something you don't know about, and it's none of your business.

"*Ja*, beautiful," Ludvík nodded.

The soldier said a few sentences in praise of various sights and monuments of Prague, but eventually he realized that Ludvík was deliberately displaying a lack of interest and he broke off in midsentence. He turned away and was about to leave, but then decided to give it one last try.

"*Also, nichts mit dem Hund?*"

"*Nichts.*"

"*Gratis?*" said the soldier.

"*Nichts,*" said Ludvík.

The poodle was quicker to depart than the soldier. It darted away in the direction of the Summer Palace and the soldier set off after it. It occurred to Ludvík that he might have been a bit more sociable, but the soldier could hardly have expected it of him. He was a stranger, and this brief conversation had been no more than an interlude in a long, misguided journey. He had traveled through the African desert and the lands of the Scythians and reached the sandy banks of the Oxus and, had it been possible, he would even have entered the land of the Britons at the very edge of the world. But it wasn't.

Ludvík saw smoke rising above the familiar rooftops and was pleased. He looked at his watch. Kamil was very late and would probably not make the rendezvous. Ludvík decided to call for him at home. As he was leaving the park through the hole in the wall, an explosion rang out in the valley below the hill. Somewhere, someone was shooting at someone.

Translated from the Czech by A. G. Brain

A Race Through Prague

Ota Pavel

WHEN THE COMMUNISTS became one of the lead-
ing parties after the war, my father joined up immediately. He
took Mother and my brothers along with him. I was the only
one too young for such matters. He joined that party of Communists enchanted, as were many others, by the Red Army.
In his case, the moment of enchantment had taken place on
the box seat of a horse-drawn wagon driven by a long-haired
Russian soldier who was giving him a ride to Buštěhrad.
Father also believed that here at last were just and decent
people who would not divide humankind up into whites and
blacks, Jews and non-Jews. At least that is what they promised in their books and speeches, all the way back to Lenin.

After their return from the concentration camp, our parents lived it up. They would go dancing in the Belvedere and
the Barbarina. The wine flowed freely, as though they were
trying to make up for all those years of privation, poverty, and
humiliation.

Arnošt Lustig used to call on us a lot in those days, because
he studied and went on sprees with my brother Jirka. Most of
all, Lustig loved to dance with Mother. He was a wonderful
dancer, like a light breeze drifting across the dance floor, and
Mother was very fond of dancing with him because my father
stamped and puffed like an elephant when he danced.
Mother was a beauty and Lustig was just a touch in love with
her. Once a handsome, fair-haired man invited her to dance

and Father nodded, indicating that Mother could dance with him. The gentleman began to woo her, and halfway through the number he told her, "You're so beautiful." He couldn't take his eyes off her. Mother laughed, for what woman wouldn't have been pleased? And then the handsome man added, "But I'm curious to know what you have in common with that Jew."

"Three children," said Mother, and she finished dancing and sat down beside Father again.

At the Belvedere my father met an American called Johnny. Johnny was beautiful, like an unspoiled maiden, and he had paws like a bear. Father always said that whenever Czech girls saw him they took their clothes off, but I was only fourteen at the time and didn't know what that meant. Today, however, I know it was mainly because there weren't many Americans in Prague and probably only one Johnny. And he really was a cool customer. He had flown fighter planes against the Germans and knocked a couple out before they shot him down and turned him into a bit of an invalid with a slight limp in his left leg. But his courage was still intact, and people would scatter when he drove his Willy's jeep through the streets of Prague. What was more, he had an important position in the United Nations Relief and Rehabilitation Administration, which was trying to help the Czechs out. His pockets were always full of dollars and he gave gallons of gas to my father and thousands of American cigarettes, sweaters, coffee, jam, and packages of chewing gum. Father accepted it as a member of the Party, and the fact that it came from an American didn't bother him a bit. Who else should accept American goods if not the Jews, who had suffered the most?

At the same time, Johnny was good-hearted. He said he

had relatives somewhere in North Bohemia and that he owned some beautiful tenement houses there and that one day he was going to manage them properly. But he never had time to go and look at the buildings himself.

The elections of 1946 were drawing near and Father took it into his head that our family should do something for the victory of Communism. His idea was that on the eve of the elections we would run through Prague. We would each wear the number of a political party and thus foreshadow by the order in which we ran the outcome of the vote. Mother declared that only Father could come up with such an idiotic idea, but Father wouldn't listen to her. Today, when I think back on it, I have to admit that Father had the right idea. It was strange, and beautiful.

Early next morning, Father disappeared with the idea of dragging Johnny back for the race, since an event like that ought to have army backing. They arrived late that afternoon, and Johnny apparently hadn't wanted to hear anything about it. But Father managed it. We didn't know how, but it was obvious that if he could sell electric vacuum cleaners in villages where they had no electricity, he could also win Johnny over. They showed up late in the afternoon. I can't remember whether the sun was shining or whether it was overcast. I only know that Johnny was a little looped. He had a bottle of whisky under the dashboard and he was mumbling something. I went close to him and heard very clearly, "Let the scurvy old world croak . . ." My father had managed to bring him around completely.

While we went to change into our T-shirts, Johnny practiced driving his jeep in circles on Farská Street, one foot on the gas, the other on the fender, smoking a cigar. He was wearing a spanking new U. S. Army colonel's uniform and he looked great in it. If a woman had walked by, I thought, she would have taken her clothes off at once. But he was waiting for us.

I had two brothers, so there were three of us. Father, naturally, was not going to run, for he was past his prime and horribly bandy-legged. For a hundred crowns and some of Johnny's American chewing gum, he had recruited a fourth boy. Mother fastened our numbers on and silently cursed Father. But Father's eyes were ablaze. He was convinced that this race would be a great achievement.

We went outside. Johnny, we discovered, had already emptied the bottle of whisky. The first to start was Hugo. He had a magnificent chest, and on it, pinned there by Father himself, was number one, the Communist Party's number in the election. Next, Father sent off the boy who was running for a hundred crowns and chewing gum. He gave him number three. My father calculated that the Social Democrats, whose number it was, would be second. Third to be sent off was Jirka, wearing number two. He represented the People's Party. Father left me till last. The Czech Socialists would be fourth. Father chose me deliberately because I was the best runner, and if something happened, I could get away fast. I had trained with the Sparta Sports Club under Father Jandera. I had strong thighs and was quick off the mark. Father Jandera predicted a great future for me as a sprinter, but I didn't have the will to train. Athletics is hard work. Father ordered me to limp a little, perhaps so I'd keep my distance from the others, and perhaps to demonstrate what miserable shape the Czech Socialist Party was in.

We ran out of Strossmeyer Square, along the Embankment

and into Příkopy Street. It didn't seem to me like such a bad idea at all. I was running almost alone through Prague, the focus of attention. The Communists clapped and the Czech Socialists jeered a little. This was neither training nor hard work. It was a strange race in which my father had decided the outcome in advance. The Communists first, the Czech Socialists last. And so it went. We were not to pass each other. Flags flapped in the windows, people were dressed to the nines and in a festive mood. I even stopped limping, thrust my chest forward, and showed off my powerful legs as they pounded along over the cobblestones. It was rather intoxicating, but my father rode behind me in the jeep with Johnny and occasionally called out, "Great! That's great! But put a little more limp into it!"

Johnny was driving along behind me. I caught sight of him three times when I stopped to pull up my socks. He was driving the very best American vehicle, the one they say won World War II. It was a Model WB, sixty horsepower, with incredible acceleration. Jeeps had been used as mine detectors, for breaking down blockades, as jiggers on the railways. And now one of them was being used to support the Communist Party in an election. The jeep had beautiful whitewall tires and there was an American star on the hood. It was like a strange, pale-green fish with bulging eyes. Johnny looked great up there, smoking his umpteenth cigar and humming something to himself, probably the same song about the scurvy old world my father had learned from the miners in Buštěhrad when he was small and sang to make Granny Malvina happy.

I don't know what possessed Father to have us run up Wenceslas Square where the Czech Socialists, for whom I was running in a limping and distant fourth place, had their headquarters. We turned out of Příkopy into the long square, and up ahead I could see a huge crowd in front of the Melantrich building. As I drew closer, my heart began to shrink. So did the aisle of people into which I was supposed to run. I looked around for my father, my last hope, yet I knew him too well to believe in that hope. He had some bad qualities but he wasn't chicken-shit, as Jews were sometimes described. He never took an insult lying down. He'd already beaten up a couple of fellows who had cursed or harmed him, and he had been to court a few times because of it. The top Jew in the world for him was neither Mr. Einstein nor Mr. Chaplin but Baer, the boxer who had knocked out Schmelling. Before the war Father had a boxing ring set up in our flat and we had to learn how to box. I was seven at the time. Mr. Hrabák but mainly Mr. Jenda Heřmánek, who won the silver Olympic medal in Amsterdam, came to coach us. But I suspected that everything I'd learned when I was seven would be useless to me now.

There was only one thing to do. Not run at all. That is what I did. My legs stopped all by themselves; I stood there and the jeep braked to a stop too. Father might have said, "Climb up with us, buddy." Up there with Johnny's uniform, in that fabulous jeep of his with its great acceleration, his genuine American Colt 45, my father's fists. But he didn't. It was Baer he loved, not Einstein. He leaned out of the jeep and gave me the order: "Run, damn it! And limp!"

My brothers and the chewing gum kid had already vanished. First I began to walk, and then in front of the Czech Socialists' headquarters I broke into a slow trot. It was interesting: until then only a few people had paid any attention to our race, but in Wenceslas Square it was different. People there understood at once what the point of the race was. They were intelligent. They were only silenced by their own astonishment at my audacity at making fun of them right in front of their own headquarters. There was a collective gasp, then a roar, and then they surged after me. A race at Strahov Stadium would have looked pale beside this. At once I stopped limping as Father had advised and began to apply the lessons of Father Jandera:

> Explode out of the blocks!
> Lift your knees high!
> Eyes straight ahead!
> Go!

It was too late. The circle closed in and the lanes were blocked with people. Up ahead, my brave brothers had vanished and the jeep with its crew was trapped somewhere behind me. Johnny blew the horn piercingly, but that was all.

There was nowhere to run and so I stopped and waited. My legs were trembling and if it could have, my heart would have leapt out of my body and started beating all by itself there on the paving stones, just so they would take pity on me. By now they were very close. Then one of them leaned forward and snatched my number off. Another hit me in the face with such force that I fell on my knees. They began to beat me. As I tried to dodge the blows, I saw their eyes. The eyes of office workers, doctors, engineers, businessmen, though the first person to hit me must have been a butcher because it was a terrible blow.

I knew those eyes. These people were beating me for those future, distorted, and half-truthful radio reports and those naive stories; they were beating me for the stupid and idiotic acts we would commit when we finally triumphed. They were beating me for our treachery and for the murders we would commit.

I got all this in advance. They ripped my shirt and shorts off and I stood there naked on Wenceslas Square, covering my groin. I was a good-looking lad then, but not good-looking enough to be able to stand proudly in the middle of Mother Prague, just as I was. A stream of blood from my nose and face trickled down over my chest and legs. Then Johnny's jeep appeared. When Johnny saw me there covered with blood, he stopped, pulled out his Colt, and walked slowly toward me through the silence. But he didn't start shooting. He stuck the Colt back in its holster, took me in his arms, and carried me back to his jeep, and the blood soaked into his beautiful uniform. Father was sitting in the other seat clenching his fists in rage.

Then Johnny drove through Prague like a madman. Back at the apartment building where we lived, he carried me into our place. When Mother saw me, her first impulse was to light into Father, whose wonderful idea all this had been. Father ran back down the stairs shouting that he was going for a doctor. Dr. Ptáček had huge spectacles and a lot of bandages. He washed me, patched me up like an inner tube, and wound me up in bandages.

The next day I didn't wake up until evening. Everything hurt and I thought I was dying. Someone was waiting humbly in my room. Through the cracks in the bandages I saw Father smiling at me. He wore a red carnation in his lapel. He said something I couldn't understand. I shook my head and he leaned close to me and repeated it. He was trying to make me feel better, perhaps even to give something to me. I saw his beaming face and finally I heard clearly what he was saying: "We won!"

Johnny was standing behind him nodding that we had indeed won, completely unaware that by this very victory he had lost those beautiful tenement houses in the north that he hadn't even looked at yet. Afterward Father told me that he had talked with Mr. Hrubý, a member of parliament, and that next year they would accept me, though I was only seventeen, as a member of the Communist Party of Czechoslovakia.

I lay there in my bed, my head aching and my neck, back, and legs swollen and sore where they had kicked me and on which I limped for a long time after that, even without my father's urging. I looked sadly at Father and wondered whether I would ever again be able to play hockey for Sparta.

At that point Johnny apologetically pulled from his bag the most wonderful shirt I had ever seen, a real American officer's khaki shirt made of fine linen, with small lions and officer's stars sewn onto it. It was cuddly, something I needed to put in bed beside me to play with like a teddy bear or a doll. I wanted to fall asleep and look forward to having it still there, and wake up, then go back to sleep, certain that no one would ever take it from me.

Then I slept for a long time as a future member of the Communist Party of Czechoslovakia with an American shirt for special occasions, and by the time I had recovered completely, the Communists had the power they had been yearning after for decades, and they began to establish order in this land.

My father did his best to help Communism overtake and surpass capitalism, as Joseph Stalin desired. He tried as hard as he could, even though a lot of Jews told him he was a *meshugge.*

The Party never entrusted him with an important position, but they did make him chairman of some entertainment committee or other, and he would walk (he no longer had his Buick) from store to store, trying to find plaster deer, gnomes, and dancing wind-up dolls for raffle prizes. When he got me into the Communist Party after I turned seventeen, I went along with him. I was impressed at the time, but when I think back on it today I can see that because of all those meetings, those raffles and public demonstrations of friendship, I never learned to dance and I had a lot fewer girlfriends than other fellows my age, which will go on haunting me for a long time to come.

He defended Communism wherever he went. His main argument to prove that we weren't going downhill and were about to overtake capitalism was that the coffee grinder in every shop was always busy. Among his close friends, he would explain that he had been a Communist before there even was a Communist Party. As a boy he had even given some poor kids muffins from the farm. On the run from the Foreign Legion, he had read to illiterate Spanish Communists from their own newspapers, though he himself couldn't speak Spanish. He had sung "Avanti Popoli" in the Fernando prison. He had had the railings and fences painted for the soccer players of the Kladno Sports Club. As a sailor on the *Tereza Taja* he had transported Russian noblewomen escaping the October Revolution, and had given them nothing but sardines to eat. When they fainted from the heat, he bathed their beautiful breasts with water. These were incontrovertible proofs, although in the last case, even though the October Revolution and that handful of sardines may have had a role to play, those beautiful aristocratic bosoms somehow didn't fit in.

But so be it! The fact is, my father was close to Communism, and he was often in the company of bums, vagrants, and poor people. And more than anything else, he had a generous heart.

When the Communists won in Bohemia, his close friend Heller, who owned a factory, told him, "You're crazy. You're even helping them out." Then Heller left for England and opened a fur-coat factory, just like the one he'd owned in Czechoslovakia. My father was no longer in business. He made a living any way he could. We became worse and worse off but the important thing for my father was that friendship, brotherhood, and above all, equality of race, existed. That was worth any money.

By that time, all our parents had left was a little house near Prague. Once I came out to visit them but I couldn't see anyone around. I entered, afraid that something had happened to them. They were in the back room. Mother was lying on the couch wrapped up in a blanket, her face turned to the wall. Father was sitting in his drawers at the table, crying. His hair had fallen over his forehead, and his tears were dripping onto the newspaper in front of him. It was *Rudé Právo*, the Communist Party daily to which he subscribed and without which he couldn't have made it through the day. I leaned over him and brushed the hair from his forehead. For the first and last time in his life he slipped into my arms, the way children do. By that time I was already a man. I held him and looked over his head at the newspaper, where he had underlined with a red pen:

> RUDOLF SLÁNSKÝ, OF JEWISH ORIGIN
> BEDŘICH GEMINDER, OF JEWISH ORIGIN
> LUDVÍK FREJKA, OF JEWISH ORIGIN
> BEDŘICH REICIN, OF JEWISH ORIGIN
> RUDOLF MARGOLIUS, OF JEWISH ORIGIN

The list of Jews went on and it was blurred with tears. When he had calmed down, he looked absently at me, as if he didn't know who I was, and said, "They're killing Jews again. They're looking for someone to blame it on all over again."

Then he stood up and punched the newspaper and shouted, "I can forgive murder — even judicial murder, even political murder. But a Communist newspaper should never print 'of Jewish origin.' The Communists are dividing people up all over again, into Jews and non-Jews."

And then he punched *Rudé Právo* again, and it fell apart as though it had been made of rotten leaves. The antique table with its inlaid deer collapsed. He sat down and sighed deeply. We all knew he was thinking about how useless all those demonstrations and flags had been, those speeches about truth and justice, how pointless had been the blood that dripped out of me onto Wenceslas Square. He was thinking too of how pointless it was that even Johnny had gone with us, that fabulous fellow who later bought himself a ranch somewhere in Texas and was raising cattle. Even the plaster deer for the raffles were pointless, and the doll in the pink skirt that danced when you wound it up. My father stood up and went into the woodshed. There he picked up the biggest ax, the one used for splitting logs. I was afraid and I went after him. Mother begged me to leave him alone; she'd never seen him like this before. After a while I pulled myself loose and ran out after him. I ran up to the gate on which he always painted a five-pointed star every May Day. Today he had carved two large stars into the wood. I stood there and counted the points: one, two, three, four, five, six . . .

I moved closer, as though I couldn't believe my own eyes. Father thought I was going to efface those Jewish stars, and he raised his ax. But I had no intention of doing that, for I understood him very well. At that gate he had ceased to be a Communist and had become a Jew once more. We looked at each other. He had something in his eyes that I had never seen there before, the terrible disappointment and despair of a man who thought he was crossing a river on a solid bridge only to discover that the bridge wasn't there at all. In those eyes too were Slánský and Margolius, swinging at the end of their ropes. All around in the dusk, birds were singing and it was like the old Jewish Psalms. He let the ax fall and sat down in his underwear in the chair that stood ready to welcome guests worn out by their journey or by life. He was expecting them to come for him too. But no one did. He had no power and he wasn't in charge of anything. He was too small a fish. At the time all he did was raise rabbits.

When I looked outside that night, he was still sitting there in the chair. A golden star was just falling, and it was more beautiful and perhaps more just than all the stars in this strange land.

Translated from the Czech by Paul Wilson

Invasion Day

Ivan Diviš

ON AUGUST 20, 1968, I bought — from whom I no longer know — a heavy-duty tape recorder. I think I paid five hundred crowns for it, and as a bonus I got a tape of Ray Charles, and I carried my load with my head down through dusty Hloubětín and up stony Poděbradská Street to our house. Why I didn't take the bus I don't know. In my idiotic hind brain I carried a dull sensation of impending misfortune, but as usual I had no idea why. A while before, in the newsroom, Frýbort had said to me, "You and a tape recorder? They don't go together. It'll amuse you for half an hour, no more." And so I bore in that beloved hind brain of mine a premonition, but it was really no more than that. In this way everyone deceives themselves. Only some know; they know ahead of time and they're suspect, or they share in the guilt, or they're out-and-out criminals.

I took the tape recorder onto the veranda. I was home alone. My wife had taken our son, Martin, to her mother's, my mother-in-law, and she was staying over and sulking, as she often did when I got into the hops somewhere in town with friends and acquaintances, with those friends of mine who were "in the arts" . . . a terrible sin . . . the unforgivable one . . . and I put the tape recorder on my beautiful baroque-rococo table — I'll never see it again — where I'd spread out everything good I'd been able to coax out of my idiotic hind

From *The Theory of Reliability.*

brain, file folders, manuscripts, a Finnish knife, books. The weather was clouding over. I took some sleeping pills and began playing Ray Charles over and over again and it amused me longer than Frýbort had predicted. I put my head in my hands and listened to that damaged, precise, deeply erotic voice of Ray Charles and his piano. . . .

I tumbled into bed, fell asleep instantly, and slept soundly, and at four o'clock in the morning the telephone rang like a band saw spinning in the air and I jumped out of bed and picked up the receiver. It was Frýbort: "The Russians have been pouring in since midnight — go outside right now! The Kbely airport's right behind your house."

I said, "Zdeněk, if this is just some dumb joke, you'll get a punch in the nose you'll never forget."

"This is no joke, man. Go outside, take a look, and then get the hell out of there!"

What I felt from this instinctive postponing of tragedy was a leaden weight about forty centimeters in diameter pressing down on my chest. I walked out on the veranda, took my rucksack, and threw the following things into it in this order: 1) the *New Testament;* 2) a stiletto knife, which I no longer have; and 3) a Tyrolean apple as beautifully green as the eyes of the most versatile mistresses, i.e. bedmates. I probably threw the knife in for the Russians. At that point, under the veranda and below where the old marquess lives, the puppy began whining and howling. We called him Mášenka, a lovable creature. He had been aroused by the rustling and rumbling overhead, but mainly he was cold. So the first thing I did under the occupation was run down the covered stairs from the veranda under the marquess, grab the puppy by the soft nape of his neck, and carry him to the wire fence of my neighbor Kubík, that son of a bitch of an informer, and drop him delicately into the flower bed not far from the doghouse belonging to his bitch, Stella, whom I'd written a poem about. Mášenka went straight into the doghouse looking for warmth.

And now at last I turned my attention to the occupation. I looked toward the airport five hundred meters away and what did I see? Monsters descending from the air, one a minute, Antonovs they call them, settling heavily onto the ground with their cargo of blunt hatred, full of steel and people who didn't know what they were doing. I did the only proper thing at that moment: I made an enormous sign of the cross, not just over my chest but over my forehead as well, and I said: So this is the end of life, which was a statement both right and wrong since I was forty-four at the time and today I'm sixty-two and I'm still alive.

I no longer remember precisely the practicalities of it, nor does it matter; I only know that I went through the garden to the gate, kicked it open, and walked with my head sunk between my shoulders — what a curse still to have a head on one's shoulders — to the Černý Bridge and in the middle of it, standing between two women with plastic handbags, some pisshead was saying in a loud voice, "What did those students think they were doing?" That was his commentary, the product of his brain, on the descending tragedy, this denouement of everything, and I suddenly realized with horror that there were other people in the world who spoke my own language and yet were different from me. And I turned right, toward the excise office, where the house stood in which we had made passionate love and then tortured each other like horses. I pushed the white doorbell and upstairs in the window the sleepy, still seductive head of my titian-haired Jindra appeared. "Jindra, get up! A terrible thing has happened. The

Russians have invaded," I shouted. "Let me in!" And upstairs
the rage was over; I embraced Jindra, and Martin emerged
from the door next to her room, still small and obviously
sleepy-eyed, with circles under his eyes. I put my arms around
him too, and all three of us stood there in the name of Jesus
. . . for wherever two or three are gathered together in My
Name, I am among you. . . .

And then, with those embraces, I left them as they were
and walked away with a single aim, to get to the editorial
offices of *Mladá Fronta*. Why, I can't tell you — force of habit,
the employment syndrome — but nothing was running, and
so I walked down the endless ash-covered path to the
Hloubětín terminus, but nothing was running there either
and so, beside myself with anger, I walked all the way to the
Harfa intersection, cursing and swearing (in this I am a master), where a Number Five going toward the center suddenly
appeared, and I jumped onto it and went all the way to Příkopy, and for some reason it went past the insurance office
where that citizen of Prague, Franz Kafka, had worked on his
files hatefully, stubbornly, and methodically — by now, everything that could possibly happen has happened in this city —
and I turned into Panská Street, got as far as the *Mladá
Fronta* office, and the gate was closed and secured with a
heavy chain (until that moment I had never known this
building had a heavy gate, and where did they suddenly get
this chain?). And there — how was it? — stood Zdeněk
Frýbort, as pale as a sheet of paper and, in a green riding
outfit, Jana N., the frigid fucker, and she kissed me and said,
"Ivan, I'm so terribly upset!" And I believed she was, and I
embraced Zdeněk and then everything began happening at
once, in rapid succession, as if in a tragicomic movie with no
director. There were four children outside the gateway into

Mladá Fronta, four Red Army soldiers in heavy scratchy over-
coats, each with a machine gun over his shoulder, and I
thumped one of them (I thumped him emphatically on the
shoulder) and I said to him, "Let me inside, man. Today's
payday." And he let me get away with it, he didn't shoot me,
but he retorted, "*Ty rabotayesh zdyes?*" and I said, "Yeah, man,
I work here. None of this is your fault and you don't even
know where you are." And suddenly I noticed something
lying across the street on the sidewalk by the wall, some mystical object, and I went over and picked it up and it was a
newspaper folded over four times and soaked with still warm
human blood. I didn't leave it there, but picked it up and took
it with me and in my idiotic hind brain I understood everything, everything. It doesn't matter *what* we understand, but
how we understand it. Of course the thing itself is also important, but above all it's how the thing is presented and how it
presents itself . . . and the dearest person we have, my teacher
Václav Černý, would back me up on this. He had to look at
this too — farewell, Professor.

   So I carried the thing, and the three of us, Frýbort, Jana,
and I, walked to the Old Town Square, and Frýbort, at other
times cool and distanced, was beside himself and periodically
shouted, "A gun! Give me a gun!" But no one gave him a gun,
no one, and so we walked down Celetná Street and suddenly,
coming toward us, was a procession and at the head of it the
dear Czechoslovak flag, spattered with blood for the last
time, and the flag was borne by an appropriately handsome
young man who I think was Martin Štěpánek, and someone
in the procession shouted, "Don't go on, the Russians are
there!" And we walked on and there it was: where Celetná
runs into the Old Town Square stood a Soviet tank jammed
across the street at an angle and in its turret stood a Red

Army soldier so filthy that even his eyes were dirty and he wasn't a Russian but a Tartar, an Asian, and at that moment the very thing that ought to be, as Emanuel Rádl says, happened and ceased to happen: I had a moment when I might have jumped on the tank and embraced the man on the turret and said to him, "Friend and brother! In the name of Christ! You're not doing a good thing, you're doing a bad thing! Love thine enemy!" It was that mystical moment that is always with us, everywhere, but Christendom disregards that moment, that instant, and yes, the moment passed, ebbed away, and once more we were those old, sinful, drunken men, those old men in the non-name of Christ, and we turned and we went nowhere, away, nowhere, helpless and utterly powerless.

How I got back to Hloubětín I don't know, but I got back. It was August 21; I walked back up Poděbradská and I saw a column of Soviet troops and tanks and who should appear at that moment but my stupid, mindless, primitive mother-in-law reeling about with my son, Martin, Martin the firstborn, the saint who shared his coat with a beggar, threading their way among the Soviet panzers, and I yelled, "You cow! The child's here!" And I dragged Martin out of the panzers' way and my mother-in-law didn't utter a word against me, for in that instant she comprehended, and I took Martin and went to our garden and started playing football with him between the house and the gate, while the war vehicles poured along the highway from the Kbely airport, crammed with idiots who had no idea who they really were or where they really were, driving down the road as though they were at home, while Martin and I played football, each trying with all his might to score. . . .

Translated from the Czech by Paul Wilson

A Visit to the Train Station

Jáchym Topol

THE CITY WAS CHANGING. Above it, as dependable as in the tenth century or any other time, the moon hung in the night's dark gateway, sometimes full and puffy like the face of a drunk, at other times floating in the clouds, almost invisible, a glassy bauble that didn't burn but still drove the city mongrels mad. Here in this glow, whenever the moon climbed to its cool intensity, lovers would drink off the last of their bottle and hurl themselves at one another, nibbling corners off love supreme, the killer would sneer as he twisted his knife in the wound, and here in this light, dear mommy would suddenly do something atrocious to her little papoose, and the golden force flowed down over the tracks of trams and trains and they glistened brilliantly in the flood of light. . . . The Lord of the Earth caught hold of the dark at its center and turned the night inside out like freshly peeled skin. Then the sun would blaze in the sky, beating down on walls and sidewalks, and only then was filth filth and decay decay, and now you could see it. The searing sun caused blood to move slowly and lazily, turn sweet, or else it made the pumps work frantically so the blood seemed ready to burst from its confines. That's how it always seemed to me, nothing pretty about it.

The city was changing. Iron grills and shutters pulled down for years and gone to rust were given fresh coats of paint and often a sign with somebody's name on it. Dusty cellars and dirty beer joints in what used to be the Jewish quarter were cleverly converted into luxury stores. You could find steamer trunks from the last century, a book dictated by Madonna herself with a piece of her chain included, pineapples and fine tobacco, diaries of dead actresses and trendy wheels from farmers' wagons, whips and dolls and travel grails with adventurer's blood in them, coins and likenesses of Kafka, shooting galleries with all the proletarian presidents as targets, rags and bones and skins, anything you could think of. In the back of one showcase were two statuettes, half-dog, half-man, stooping under heavily laden wicker baskets, their glassy eyes watching you over their shoulders, and maybe they even knew your name. They were statuettes of the Devil, and they sat there for a long time before anyone bought them. I was relieved when they finally disappeared, but next day in their place stood a cat-woman figurine with green eyes, inlaid precious stones, and raven-black hair. The hair was human and she was just as eerie. Pozener, the company that owned the store, was from Vienna and their logo had the horns of a bull in it.

The city was changing. Old broken walls were torn down, ads were pasted up over cracked, mysterious maps in the roughcast plaster, sidewalks were newly paved, barriers of sheet metal and wood left standing for years vanished overnight. New owners took charge of dilapidated buildings and tried to change them into hotels, pubs, wholesale glass and crystal shops, travel agencies. Pants, coats, wooden toys, frankfurters, newspapers, gingerbread, and gold were sold on the street out of ground-floor apartments, and the idea of declaring income was a joke. Nothin' sleazy about money, the

sleazeballs said, and they parceled up the streets and squares
to fit the size of their stands. On the periphery of the city and
in the outlying districts, new centers sprang up around discos,
mini department stores, new bars, and restaurants. Evenings,
the laundromat on our street filled up with mothers. —Told
me I was nothin' but his landlady now, so I give him the
heave-ho and now he don't live nowhere. —Mine'll come
home plastered today; last time he went out for groceries,
time he got back the food was rotten. —Here're your shirts,
sir, she told me, giving me the eye to get lost. —Yeah, fine,
you're short, but come up with the money by the first of the
month or you're out one bathrobe. —He don't eat that stringy
meat, I heard another say.

But it wasn't enough to quench my thirst for life. I searched
for a way to wear out my vigorous mind on business activities,
worked my way up to literary mercenary, a dealer in words, a
street-smart hack. Most of the people in the neighborhood
were more successful. Dunar the crook, blackmailer, and
wino became lord of Nightland, a disco that reeked with the
stench of burnt flesh from the hot rocks tossed from one ma-
fioso clientele to the next. Come again sometime, Dunar told
the emissary from one of those nasty foreign outfits that
came to Prague to harvest in the fields of gold. Come again,
he told the wise-ass who confidently demanded a premium
for protection, and I'll kill you. They shot the guy the next
week; he probably came just to have himself some fun, and
they didn't give him a chance to trot out his offer a second
time. Show this to mommy, Dunar told the guy's date as he
expertly snapped her collarbone in two. Then his gorillas
worked her over a little bit more, just enough so she'd barely

survive, and tossed her onto a garbage heap outside of town, all rolled up in the crime-flecked carpet along with the dead protection specialist.

Stumbling by Nightland back to my dump at about 6:00 A.M. I saw Dunar perched on the hood of his BMW, just having breakfast. Three or four half-drunk flunkies were prancing around him with a bravura worthy of a changing of the guard, serving him up roast chicken and salads, gold-plated toothpicks, baskets and dishes, shots and bottles, the air pulsing with the sounds of good old ABBA. Dunar let out a belch and flung a bottle of wine at me. —Scram, scribbler, he roared, and I made myself scarce. Some time back he had asked me to write him a few pieces in praise of his "entertainment paradise," and even though I was paid a king's ransom I still hadn't turned them in. Apparently he hadn't lost faith in my genius, because the bottle smashed against the wall about five yards wide of me and none of his Dobermans came snorting for my throat.

The factory workers were walking to work with last night's hangover in the crook of their necks. —Hey Franta, Dunar greeted them, —Hey Luboš, hey Ládín, how's tricks? Nothing mean about the way he said it, and his BMW sat sparkling like a big black beetle, the hood supporting the load of deli fare without damage. Dunar was obviously having himself a ball with his flunkies and bodyguards. The working stiffs smiled, their innards invisible, but they knew that he knew that they knew. They were of one blood. Plain and simple, the master has come to town to take the chair out from under your rear, the soup from under your spoon, and shove it right in your eye. The master's going to make slaves of your sons and what's more, he's going to take his followers, your daughters and wives, and sell 'em on the street, flesh by the pound. —Hey Miloš, hey Jožín, you sonuvagun, ciao guys, ciao ciao. Onetime classmates and buddies and cagemates and workmates from the factory, onetime brothers from school, church, the Party, the army. Was a time they lived together, side by side, so to speak, fist with fist, idle gossip going hand in hand with ratting to the cops. Nowadays they just swallow hard on their spit, on their envy and hate. One day one of them is going to break Dunar's head open. Maybe soon, maybe not: when the time is right.

The city peeled off the stern and gloomy face, the mask of rotting bolshevism, and replaced it with a thousand others. Some were the smiley makeup faces of clowns, and who'd give a damn if those wacky old circus-ring alcoholics smelling of sawdust and animal dung tried to hide a few pockmarks here and there, or a two-bit scar from a two-bit stab wound? Bright-colored buffoon kissers painted on for rowdy youngsters, for female sightseers from around the globe, for the first shy kisses and fleeting touches, for the first marijuana cigarette in the mysterious twilight of foreign lands wrapped in a web of legends, for wanna-be artists in a haze of romance, rust under their nails from the iron curtain, behind which — at long last! — no more tank parades, just Punch and Judy shows for sons and daughters from well-to-do families with fabulous passports who came to Eastern Europe to go wild. Expecting a menagerie and they found a jungle, expecting a jungle and they found a warehouse of scrapped stage scenery, searching for the spirit and the mirror-faced boogeyman got them . . . for dour intellectual females who cast off Morrison and Kerouac at the age of seven, then the existentialists and the phenomenologists between eleven and sixteen . . . and all that junk and then drugs and then, once cleansed, they loved Jesus so they could start up with some other male, the harpies, and then they were men-haters with well-rounded views on what was nonconformist and environmental and witchy and lesbian, and they wore out their resigned and scornful Czech landladies with opinions delivered in words, words, words. . . . Sooner or later every lunatic with a couple of bucks, a worldview, and a vision set down in this city and founded organizations or movements or newspapers, or pulled into town with never-ending cables wrapped round their waist for the new TV, something you can look at for a change, creating CUL-TURE, or at least some cute little sect for the local suckers, or some limited liability company; after all, it's nothin' but paper, right? . . . And when the money ran out, they vanished. The city and its speculators sucked them up like a sponge.

It just about killed me too, this city . . . evenings with the fortune-teller . . . new owners tailored other parts of town into a respectable business suit, banks and foreign exchange offices, varicolored flags fluttered over the ruins and hired guns took potshots at pigeons with air rifles so their cloacal ammunition wouldn't disturb the digestion of the suits . . . and still other city districts contorted into the professional spic-and-span face of the cardshark, the try-hard, the type who's born to lose in spite of his agile fingers and lifelong practice, because he's sick, condemned by nature, a weak piece. Some streets still made you feel like the best thing to do was drug yourself till you dropped. And in some corners, dark and damp with black sewer water, you could come down with schizophrenia as easily as you catch a cold. Then again, other places seemed to emerge from the magic spell of inertia to reconnect with happier days. By some miracle, or maybe it figures, these were the oldest places, like the cathedral with the Czech kings' tombs in it and the low-flying pigeons, the sparrows and the lazy swallows outside, who move — as I like to put it, even though it might sound unusual for birds — with sublime sensuality, or the monastery with the abbot they tortured so many times.

I was walking through South Station with a hangover, examining the colorful covers of pocket novels, detective stories, and pornography, their titles resonating in the slow-motion ache of my brain, and they are points on a world map too: Here are lions. And here's *A Thousand Sex Slaughters* and here's *Black Mary* and here's *House of Spiders* and here's *Mutiny of the Robots,* and if you stand on your tiptoes you can also catch a glimpse of *Cooked Alive,* a novella, and *The Maid's Dream* and *Reign of the Fist* and *Street of Terror.* Next to that a vegetable stand, and the heavy aroma of Asian unknowns — and dill and oregano and cinnamon and olives piquant and lemons and raisins — forms a unique smell screen wafting toward *King of the Mutants* and *Maneater,* and next to that the toilets stink. The private newsdealer runs them too, besides selling porno videos.

I'm standing there pissing into the trough, watched by the paper eye of a painted slut, her legs spread wide on the cover of *Teenage Prostitute.* —You like to beat off? says the guy standing next to me. My hungover brain fails to issue the command for a lightning punch in the face, so I go on standing there and, —Huh? I ask, starting to play stupid. It's the pissoir owner himself who addressed me, an entrepreneur. Could he too be setting up some sort of movement or center? How to Change Your Life, In Harmony with Yourself, How to Get Rich, German in One Hour, Lose Weight in Three Days of Gorging, etc.? —Yeah, I see you round here, he goes on. —I work next door here, I explain, so he won't think I'm a Snooper, but he probably does anyway. —You like to beat off? —Beat what? I reply, giving him my best baffled, innocent look. He tosses a glance toward the door to make sure no one's coming and: —Just between us, if you like to beat off we could make a deal on a peep show. —Huh? —Yeah, all you do is beat off in one of the stalls and they watch. —Who? —Come off it, perverts, for Chrissake. So it's strictly a business deal between two grown-up men. Nothing happens to you, they just look. How many times can you beat it all the way? Listen, you got long hair, I stick a helmet with horns on that mop of yours and it's instant Viking. —Uh-uh, I groan. —Don't make too much where you work, do you? he says with a disapproving look at my shabby suit, but he's from the sticks, what does he know, this cotton here is brand-name. —Sorry, I tell him, doesn't grab me, and I leave him standing there, no coin tossed into his little plastic dish.

I watch the swarm of nomads inside the train station. No wonder the bushes out front are such fierce competition for the public toilets if he goes around hassling every Viking like that. Cash. How much would he have given me anyway? With that filthy mug of his, I'll bet he does the really kinky stuff himself. Helmet with horns? Yeah, right, just the thing to make it easier for the rent-a-cops to nab me! Cash, cash, cash. But there sure isn't any point in money-making without a pinch of excitement thrown in, can't argue with that.

I had a real soft spot for South Station. It was a throwback to the times when train stations got the same kind of respect airports get nowadays. Art nouveau metal holding up the vaulted ceiling, holding together the glass. Pink and green flowers so high up in the corners that the miniature drawings engraved on them were impossible to make out. Back then maybe artisans still believed that God could see their creations. At least some of them were careful, that's for sure. No freethinker could've come up with spirals like those, look at how they all coil around each other. Then again, I thought, maybe it's some kind of Freemason symbolism, and I stood there following it up into infinity till it gave me the chills. Then suddenly, out of the darkness and mist of the cosmic tunnel I was so happily tumbling into, appeared the image of Jules Verne. On one of my better days, I had traded some idiot a carton of Gauloises for a Jules Verne daguerreotype by Rondé. Afterward the guy's older brother just about killed him for being so stupid and they came to plead for it back, but I didn't budge an inch: a deal's a deal, even in bestial times. The wooden doors on the restrooms were also art nouveau: the hinges with nymphs, the hasps and mountings, as big as about six of those chipboard slabs that pass for doors nowadays. As if they'd been built for men of gigantic stature. In fact it was like the entire train station had been built for some race now long extinct. If any of those titans actually turned up here, the local riffraff would no doubt turn tail and head for the hills, and I wouldn't be far behind. But those consummate carpenters from the other end of the century left behind no holes in their work.

I still wanted to go to the waiting room and admire the enormous tiled stove for a while. Back then, the red monsters set up a Proletariat Corner in the place, and I used to spend time there, the only visitor, in quiet meditation. I fortified myself with a cup of coffee from the stand in front of the station, and just as the ticking clock in my brain was getting bearable I spotted a familiar face on a bench: —Hey, Mičinec!

Mičenec had enough years on me to have burned me more than once: I'd traded him my father's watch for some pieces of broken bottle, he'd slashed me with his skates over the Maskalířová girl, snapped my Little Bison bow in two, burned me with his lighter, ratted on me, accused me, laid the blame on me for everything that ever got broken or stolen in the building where we lived with our families. But now our fathers had crumbled to dust and the remnants of our families were scattered throughout institutes, studio apartments, and boneyards. That watch would look pretty old-fashioned these days, and that fetching red-haired creature had probably turned into a fiery old hag by now anyway, so let bygones be bygones: —How goes it, Mičinec? Sitting twisted up on the bench, he was grumbling something to himself, left hand pressed to his side. He turned my way, his eyes pure panic, then threw his head skyward, tensed up, fell silent. His hand slid from the bench, his side was covered with blood.

Translated from the Czech by Alex Zucker

Tenor Sax Solo
from Washington

Josef Škvorecký

THE PRESIDENT was scheduled to arrive at the Reduta jazz club at ten to play the sax, but it was nine-fifteen and he still hadn't shown up. The advance security men hadn't shown up either. There was only a military helicopter circling the center of Prague, sweeping the baroque gables with a spotlight, looking for snipers. Lubomír Dorůžka, the doyen of Czech jazz critics who had put out an underground swing magazine called *O.K.* during the Nazi occupation, remarked gloomily that he hoped we weren't waiting for Godot. Then a rumor went round among the assembled jazzmen. Actually there were two versions of it. The president had gone from the Castle to the Golden Tiger beer hall where he was supposed to have a beer with Bohumil Hrabal, the legendary Czech author of *Closely Watched Trains* and *Too Loud a Solitude*. But Bohumil, to calm his nerves, had fortified himself for his encounter with the president in several other beer halls and got lost, and the president couldn't find him at the Tiger. According to the second version, the people responsible for the president's movements around Prague got the Golden Tiger mixed up with the Black Ox, and when the man from Washington and his indeterminate entourage of bodyguards arrived at the Ox, he sat down for a beer, not with Bohumil Hrabal, but with Karel Pecka, who's a regular there. So the well-informed president had a beer with him, and congratulated the sixty-six-year-old novelist for looking so young at eighty. That explained the delay.

Because I've been associating with musicians for decades, I know that though they do not lie, they don't tell the truth either; they just like shooting the breeze, so I didn't believe their surrealistic explanations for the president's tardiness. And it was a good thing I didn't, because shortly after the rumor, the story, whatever it was, had gone through the establishment like a fire in dry grass, both presidents, the American and the Czech, stepped into the room.

The Reduta is one of the oldest jazz clubs in Prague. Shortly after Stalin's death they held "text appeals" by Jiří Suchý and Ivan Vyskočil. These events were a Czech specialty that depended on the combined effects of jazz and the spoken word. In the early sixties the jazz quartet, S+H Kvartet, began playing regular gigs here. The group was founded by the now-deceased vibraphonist Karel Velebný and the baritone sax player Jan Konopásek. The last time I saw Konopásek in Prague was at one of the weddings of the jazz singer Eva Olmerová, where he played the flute, but shortly after that he vanished over the hills and ended up in America. At least that's what I thought when the president's advance bodyguards walked through the door.

Before they arrived, the Czech president's bodyguards were in charge of security. Using a metal detector, one of them discovered an object in my pocket and asked me somewhat sheepishly to show him what it was. It was a tin figurine of the Virgin Mary. I had bought it many long years ago on the holy mount in South Bohemia, and I used it as a good luck charm on my frequent flights across North America. I explained this to the man, but because Czech has no expression for these accoutrements beloved of the superstitious, I used an English term for it: "*To je můj* lucky piece," I said. For a long time, he turned the object over warily in his fingers — he was clearly a product of the atheistic school system under Communism — and finally decided that it wasn't a weapon, gave it back to me, and let me into the room.

The president's security team poured into the Reduta. By Prague standards it was a colorful crowd, with a lot of women in it both black and white, and they weren't token women either, for it seemed to me that, as in life, they were in the majority. The president beckoned one of them to him, whispered something in her ear, she in turn whispered to a male colleague, and a clutch of broad-shouldered men swept into the men's room. But they weren't after a hidden assassin; it was just the consequence of the beer he'd drunk. The president left his opposite at their table and disappeared into the washroom, while the Czech president took advantage of his momentary absence to light up a cigarette. The Reduta is not yet — and probably never will be — a smoke-free zone.

Meanwhile, on the podium, the Czecho-Slovak phantasmagoric band led by the tenor saxophonist Štěpán Markovič started playing. The Slovak, Juraj Barto, drove his trumpet through a rising arc of syncopated thirty-second notes into the stratosphere, while Robert Balcar, a countryman of mine from the eastern Bohemian border regions, underlined this American music on his bass in a style that was straight out of the legendary days of my novels *The Cowards* and *The Engineer of Human Souls*. They were followed shortly afterward by the Spiritual Kvintet. Their otherworldly rendition of "Wings over Jordan" sounded to me just the way I remember hearing it on a shortwave radio at night under the German

Protectorate. The gentleman from Washington came back from the bathroom, and I suspect he felt right at home.

Then he got up on the podium and looked around for an instrument, but all he could see was something that looked like a monstrance draped in cloth. The Czech president put out his cigarette and added the butt to the seven others he had managed to get through during his colleague's absence, then he too stepped up on the podium, pulled a string, and the cloth fell away to reveal a magnificent golden tenor sax. In presenting it to the president, the Czech president proudly declared it was a Czech-made product.

And he had something to be proud of. After changing the reed, the instrument, under the American president's skillful fingers, sounded almost virtuoso — or so it seemed to me — and certainly professional, as one of the band leaders present told me, a man who had just recorded, for the film version of my *Swell Season*, the old song "I'll Lock Up Today" by poor Fritz Weiss of the Ghetto Swingers, who played his last song on the ramp at Auschwitz.

Afterward, of course, people said the president could only play "Summertime" and "My Funny Valentine," and maybe they were right: you can't expect too much of presidents, after all. Once I heard the Czech president sing a Czech folk song called "Ach synku, synku" — "Oh My Son, My Son" — and at least the American president knows how to play "Summertime."

But I have to confess that rather than listening to the president, I focused my attention on the man with the baritone sax who, as soon as the president started playing, emerged from the wings, jumped onto the bandstand without asking permission, and joined in. The last time I had

seen this man was — my god! — about twenty years ago in a
Toronto swing dance hall called the Palais Royale, with
paintings of Benny Goodman and Glenn Miller on the wall.
That time, however, no one danced, for the headliner was a
magnificent big band full of virtuosos. The least technically
skillful of them was the band leader, Woody Herman, but he
completely made up for what he lacked in technique with his
great swing soul. It was, I think, his last Herd, and with him,
in the sax section, playing a solo full of wonderful, inventive
riffs, was the man now swinging with the president. He had
gone to America before I had, a couple of days after Eva
Olmerová's wedding; he'd gone through the Berkelee School
of Music, and after a stint with Herman, he'd spent the next
thirty years plying the seven seas with an orchestra on a love
boat. The jazz fans of Prague, however, had not forgotten
him, this old friend of mine, Jan Konopásek.

So perhaps I will be forgiven for not listening to the Washington sax player as attentively as I might have. Memories
were rushing through my head, and then Konopásek played
a taped version of his combination of "The Star-Spangled
Banner" and the Czech national anthem, "Where is My
Homeland?" and the two anthems went together like a
charm. So I felt good in the Reduta, with the president of a
great democracy that I had always sworn by, and the Czech
president, surrounded by jazzmen, who had triumphed so
magnificently over forty years of an obscurantism that had
once even tried to ban the saxophone.

Translated from the Czech by Paul Wilson

The Spirit of Prague

Ivan Klíma

A CITY IS LIKE A PERSON: if we don't establish a
genuine relationship with it, it remains a name, an external
form that soon fades from our minds. To create this relationship, we must be able to observe the city and understand its
peculiar personality, its "self," its spirit, its identity, the circumstances of its life as they evolved through space and time.

Many studies and essays have been written about the spirit
of Prague. Books have come out with titles like *Magic Prague*
or *Prague, the Mystical City*. The interesting thing is that
these books were written by foreigners. The finest and best
informed book about Prague I have ever read was written
by an Italian, A. M. Ripellino; others have been written by
Prague Germans or Jews who, for the most part, had to
emigrate from Czechoslovakia to escape the Nazis. Their
portraits of Prague, it would seem, have dominated the
imaginations of many visitors to my native city. It is the portrait of a mysterious and exciting city that has inspired people's creativity by its ambiance, by the remarkable and
stimulating blend of three cultures that lived side by side for
decades, even centuries: the Czech, German, and Jewish cultures. "Ich bin hinternational," punned the German-speak-
ing Prague native Johannes Urzidil. To him, the milieu of
Prague had a fairy-tale beauty precisely because you could
live here "beyond nationality," because conflicts of nationality canceled each other out and gave birth to a kind of imma-

terial, indefinable, mysterious world, a space that could be considered neither Czech, nor German, nor Jewish, nor even Austrian. Urzidil, like many of his contemporaries, drew his picture of Prague and its streets teeming with strolling city-dwellers, but he also depicted a Prague of picturesque empty lanes, nightclubs, open-air stages, theaters and cabarets, tiny shops, small cafes, and above all, beer halls and taverns, student societies and literary salons, and of course brothels and the colorful metropolitan underworld. Of course, this portrait was dominated by the experience of his generation, but also by the remarkable number of great spirits who lived here at the turn of the century. Think only of the composers Dvořák and Smetana, the writers Hašek, Kafka, Rilke, Werfel, Urzidil, Brod, and the politician Masaryk. The Czech and German theaters were enlivened by a generation of great actors and singers; Albert Einstein lectured at the German university, and the Czech Charles University, after a long, arid period, could pride itself in a great many scholars with worldwide reputations in their field. Such an agglomeration of brilliant creative spirits cannot, of course, be explained by external circumstances, for such circumstances contribute only a place in which brilliance can express itself. But in its dying years, the Austrian empire did provide sufficient room for free creation, and that spirit, as if in anticipation of the impending catastrophe, permeated the life of the city.

But to my mind it was not freedom that most influenced the shape and the spirit of Prague, it was the unfreedom, the life of servitude, the many ignominious defeats and cruel military occupations. Prague as it was at the turn of the century no longer exists, and those who might have remembered that period are no longer alive. Jews murdered, Germans banished, many great personalities driven out and scattered across the world, small shops and cafes closed: this was the heritage Prague brought to the new fin de siècle.

Of course the spirit that prevailed at the end of the last century and the beginning of this one no longer exists anywhere in the world. It's just that elsewhere, the transition was less drastic, and less obvious. But what kind of spirit prevails in the present city?

Prague was chosen as a capital city by the Přemyslid dynasty. The territory they ruled from here was not large, but its geographical position in the middle of Europe destined it to be a place where many foreign interests would clash. Very soon after the beginning of recorded history, the Czechs were joined by others: first by the Jewish people, and, in the thirteenth century, by Germans. They all lived under a common ruler in a land for which the German language had a special word that did not exist in Czech: "Boehmen." Unlike later interpretations influenced by the nationalisms of the nineteenth and twentieth centuries, the original sources tell us that for the most part the Czechs and the German colonists got along well together, whether they lived in the border regions or right in the capital city. The lives of the Jews were more precarious, and the hate-mongers who from time to time vented their rage against them sometimes spoke Czech and sometimes German. Otherwise, all those who lived in the land suffered equally during plagues and wartime.

There was scarcely a war in Europe that did not affect the Czech state. Prague was frequently besieged and occupied, yet despite this, or perhaps because of it, negotiation and even capitulation came, in more recent centuries, to be given preference over fighting back. Such policies (often criticized) have enabled the city to survive, though not without losses.

In 1620, when the Czech aristocracy squandered their independence in an unsuccessful uprising against the Hapsburg dynasty, the country lost for the next three centuries even the degree of freedom it had enjoyed until then. Prague was plundered by the occupying forces, but it was also plundered by those who ruled over it. Almost nothing is left of the magnificent art collections assembled under Rudolf II, although at the beginning of the seventeenth century they had been among the most valuable and extensive in the world. Part of the collections were carted away to Vienna after Rudolf's death, and shortly after that much of it was taken as booty by the Swedes (one of the many who have taken Prague). What was left was gradually removed to Vienna by subsequent Hapsburg rulers.

But the material damage was only part of the misfortune that befell the city. The Protestant clergymen were exiled from the land, and most of the gentry left too. Government, education, and even the custody of people's souls, fell into the hands of foreigners. Once the seat of kings and a center of humanistic scholarship, Prague was to become a holiday resort for the court of Vienna. A city that was the first in Europe to lead the resistance to the Catholic Church was to be catholicized as quickly as possible, by force if necessary.

One of the epithets most frequently applied to Prague is the expression "the city of a hundred spires." Few people realize that many of its steeples and baroque cathedrals were built in this period of catholicization, a time that for many is associated with violence, enforced exile, a loss of homeland, or at least a loss of one's original religion.

At the same time, however, it cannot be claimed that the city suffered only losses. New preachers of the faith came and built new churches, new rulers built new palaces for themselves, and all this helped create a livelihood for the burghers and the simple people of Prague. It was during this period, in fact, that the most admired palaces and gardens were designed and erected by the best architects of European baroque.

And yet something had been broken. Something of that defeat must have affected the spirit of the city, and must have done so in a permanent way, for except for several short periods, that defeat, that loss of freedom, that subjugation to foreign rulers, was never undone. Instead, in ever quickening succession, came new defeats and new losses. Yet it is part of the mystery of this city that it was able to extract something positive from even so unfortunate a fate.

One of the most striking features of Prague is its lack of ostentation. Franz Kafka (like many other intellectuals) used to complain that everything in Prague was small and cramped. He almost certainly meant the circumstances of life, but it is also true of the city itself, its physical dimensions. Prague is one of the few big cities where, in the center, you will not find a single tall building or triumphal arch, and where even many of the palaces, though magnificent inside, put on an inconspicuous and plain face, almost like military barracks, and seem to be trying to look smaller than they really are. At the end of the last century, the people of Prague built a sort of copy of the Eiffel Tower, but they reduced it to a fifth of the original size. In the period between the two world wars, they built dozens of schools, gymnasiums, and many hospitals, but they did not build a grandiose parliament building like the ones in London, Budapest, or Vienna. In 1955 the Communists erected a gigantic monument to the Soviet dictator Joseph Stalin; seven years later, they destroyed it.

What at the beginning of the century might still have been felt as pettiness or provinciality, we perceive today rather as a human dimension, miraculously preserved.

A sense of proportion permeated the life of people as well. Czech life does not go in for a great deal of ostentation, for Barnum & Bailey-sized ads, fireworks, dazzling society balls, casinos, or grand military parades. It tends rather toward markets, seasonal festivals, and simple dances. The showiest celebration used to be the Sokol gymnastic meets, held in what at the time was the largest sports stadium in the world (it was built on the outskirts of the city so that its vastness would not be disruptive). Such events brought together tens of thousands of participants who would perform synchronized gymnastic routines in front of audiences approaching two hundred thousand. But even events like this were more an expression of moderation and disciplined enthusiasm than of a longing to amaze the world.

A history that unfolds peacefully seems to flow somewhere beyond people's awareness, but a history full of uprisings and reversals, occupations, liberations, betrayals, and new occupations enters the life of people and cities as a burden, as a constant reminder of life's uncertainties. Prague does not have many public monuments or memorials, but it does have many buildings in which innocent people were imprisoned, tortured, or executed, and they were usually the best people in the country. It is part of Prague's restraint that it does not display these wounds, as though it wished to forget about them as quickly as possible. That is why they are always tearing down monuments to those who symbolized the most recent epoch (monuments to the emperors and to the first, second, and now even the fourth president, monuments raised to honor conquerors). As well, streets are constantly being renamed. There are places in Prague that have had a change of name five times in this century alone. Strangers can walk the streets oblivious to this; a visitor who knows an area can be confused by it and wonder if he has gone astray. Street signs with new names testify to an attempt to purge the city of something it cannot be purged of — its own past, its own history, a history that seems too great a burden to bear.

For a person to bear the burden of his own destiny, and a nation the burden of its own history, patience and perseverance are necessary. A city, too, must have these qualities. In Czech, as in many other languages, the word for "patience" *(trpělivost)* has the same root as the verb to "suffer" *(trpět)*. This city, apparently spared the ravages of war, has had to bear greater suffering than many cities directly affected by belligerent action. Unlike foreigners, whose journey usually takes them only to places accessible to tourists, I have been able to enter old buildings and some former palaces and see how self-appointed, barbaric caretakers allowed ceilings to collapse or ran new walls through magnificent salons and transformed them into company canteens or offices. I have seen terraced gardens that were among the most beautiful in Europe eaten away by the damp, untended flower beds left to die, churches turned into warehouses and finally into spaces unsuitable even for storage. If Prague is still standing, and has not yet lost its allure or its beauty, it is because its very stones, like its people, have expressed their patient perseverance.

I have often wondered which place in Prague could be considered its symbolic center. The Castle? The Old Town Square? Wenceslas Square? The Castle, although it is the most common image on postcards and is most often rendered by artists, symbolizes something different for me, as I will shortly explain. Wenceslas Square, which was a marketplace until the nineteenth century, lacks an intimate historical connection with the fate of the city. And the Old Town Square? Without a doubt it embodies the burden of Czech history. For almost four centuries it has been marked by the ignominious public execution of twenty-seven Czech noblemen, burghers, and spiritual leaders in 1621. It has become a symbol of humiliation, human duplicity, and the fickle adaptability of the Prague people. Time and time again, celebrations have been held on this spot to honor the current rulers, whether loved or (more commonly) unloved, and enough people have always been found to come out and pay homage, either out of interest, or because they were driven by fear.

For me, the material and spiritual center of the city is a bridge. The almost seven-hundred-year-old stone bridge joining the river's west bank with the east as it were symbolizes the place of this city in Europe, the two halves of which have been seeking each other out at the very least since the bridge's foundations were laid. The west and the east. Two branches of the same culture, yet representing two differing traditions, different tribes of the peoples of Europe.

The Charles Bridge also symbolized, as it were, the peculiar invulnerability of this city, its capacity to recover from all disasters. For centuries, it has withstood the high waters that regularly inundated Prague. Only once, two centuries ago, did the floods destroy two of its arches, which collapsed, taking pedestrians with them, into the swollen waters. But the bridge was quickly repaired and today the citizens of Prague no longer know anything about an event that contemporary chroniclers considered one of the worst catastrophes to ever afflict the city.

The language spoken in Prague is unostentatious as well. It is full of the vernacular, and places no great store by grand emotions, as Russian does, for instance. A Czech writer today would hesitate to write that his city were "magical," or "mystical"; in fact, he would hesitate even to think so.

When Václav Havel tried, in his play *Audience*, to give a name to the situation of a banned writer who has to work in a brewery, he used the refrain: "Them's the paradoxes, eh?" The word "paradox" also applies to the spirit of this city. Prague is full of paradoxes. It is brimming with churches, yet only a small number of practicing Christians can be found in the city; it is proud of having one of the oldest universities in central Europe, and a population that has been literate for centuries, but there are few places in the world where learning is so insultingly underrated.

Another paradox is the structure that dominates the city: the Prague Castle. It is one of the largest fortresses in Central Europe (its basic ground plan was established before the era of grand defeats), a great castle that went through its last great reconstruction at a time when the ruler scarcely lived in it at all. Now it is the seat of presidents. Their fate reflects the fate of the city from which they ruled the country. Of the nine previous presidents, four spent more than three years in prison; a fifth was in prison for a shorter time; another (perhaps better forgotten, since most of his presidency coincided with the period of Nazi occupation) died in prison, and the three remaining escaped prison or execution only by fleeing the country. What a strange and paradoxical connection between prisons and the royal castle!

It is perhaps only in a city so full of paradoxes that, within the space of several weeks, two vastly different but brilliant writers could have been born. One was a Jew who would write in German, a vegetarian and teetotaler and self-absorbed ascetic, a man almost obsessed with the knowledge of his own responsibility, his mission as a writer, his own shortcomings, so much so that he would not dare publish most of his works during his lifetime. The other was a drunk, an anarchist, a bon vivant, an extrovert who loved being irresponsible, who ridiculed his profession and his responsibilities, who would write in pubs and sell his work on the spot for a few beers. Franz Kafka and the author of *The Good Soldier Švejk* both died prematurely within a year of each other, separated by only a few streets. Both drew on the same period to create works of genius, but those works seem separated not just by ages but by continents as well. Because the word paradox is a rather grand-sounding word, or at least one smelling of intellectualism, people would, from that time on, call the absurd situations life puts them in a *Kafkárna* and would call their own ability to make light of such situations, to confront violence with humor and utterly passive resistance *Švejkovina*.

The Prague of past eras is gone. No one will raise the murdered ones from the dead, and most of those who were driven out will probably never come back to live. Nevertheless, Prague has survived and finally, after a long time, has tasted freedom again. Its spirit has survived as well. This manifested itself vividly during the revolution that opened the way to freedom in 1989. Revolutions are usually marked by high-sounding slogans and many flags, and blood flows, or at least glass is shattered and stones fly. The November revolution which earned the epithet "velvet" differed from standard revolutions not only in its nonviolence, but chiefly in the main weapon used in the struggle. It was ridicule. Almost every available space in Prague — the walls of buildings, the subway stations, the windows of buses and streetcars, shop windows, lampposts, even statues and monuments — were covered, in the space of a few days, with an unbelievable number of signs and posters. Although the slogans had a single object — to overthrow the dictatorship — their tone was light rather than serious. They employed irony and ridicule. The citizens of Prague delivered the coup de grace to their despised rulers not with a sword, but with a joke. Yet at the heart of this original, unemotional style of struggle there dwelt a stunning emotionality. It was, for the time being, the most recent and perhaps the most remarkable paradox in the life of this remarkable city.

Translated from the Czech by Paul Wilson

A Prague Chronology

A.D. 7TH CENTURY According to legend, the Slavic princess, Libuše, has a vision of a great city. She marries Přemysl, a simple plowman. They build a fortress overlooking the Vltava River and their descendants rule over the Czech kingdom until 1306.

A.D. 935 Václav, or Wenceslas, the Přemyslid duke celebrated in the popular carol, is murdered by his brother, becoming the country's patron saint. His remains are reputedly buried beneath the rotunda in St. Vitus Cathedral.

10TH–14TH CENTURY The Czech kingdom becomes a prosperous electorate in the Holy Roman Empire, and Prague a major trading and ecclesiastical center with significant German and Jewish communities.

1346–1378 The Czech king, Charles IV, becomes Holy Roman Emperor. Prague enters a Golden Age; in 1348 Charles University is founded; the Nové Město (New Town) is built; work begins on the Charles Bridge, linking the two banks of the Vltava; the Cathedral of St. Vitus rises adjacent to the abutments of the Prague Castle; scholars and artists flock to the imperial court.

1389 The Easter Pogrom. Three thousand Jews are murdered in the Jewish ghetto.

1415 Jan Hus, a prominent Prague theologian and preacher, is burnt at the stake in Constance for heresy. His teachings provoke widespread dissent against the power of the Catholic Church.

1419 The Hussites cast thirteen anti-reformist burghers from the windows of the New Town Hall, triggering a general uprising and foreshadowing the Reformation and the great wars of religion. During a century of political upheaval, the importance of Prague is eclipsed by Vienna.

1576–1611 Emperor Rudolf II restores Prague as capital of the Holy Roman Empire. Rudolf attracts distinguished men of letters to the imperial court; the influence of the Italian Renaissance is reflected in architecture and the visual arts. Prague becomes a center for the study of science and the occult — in particular, alchemy and the quest for gold. The Rabbi Loew (1512–1609), legendary creator of the Golem, is the spiritual leader of the Jewish community.

1618 Angry Protestants turn on the Catholic deputies of Prague and the second defenestration takes place in the Old Town Square, leading to an outbreak of hostilities which eventually embroils all of Europe in the Thirty Years War.

1620 Protestant Bohemian forces are routed by the Imperial Army at the Battle of White Mountain in present-day Břevnov. Twenty-seven leaders of the uprising are publicly executed in the Old Town Square. In the wake of the humiliation of the Bohemian and Moravian independence movements, the stamp of Hapsburg power is imprinted on the city in a profusion of baroque architecture — massive churches, elaborate palaces, and ornate monuments. German becomes the official language.

1787 Mozart premieres *Don Giovanni* in the Stavovské Theater. Despite political obscurity, Prague's vitality as a cultural center is not extinguished. The city becomes a mecca for musicians and composers. Italian opera and choral music flourish.

1791 Mozart premieres *The Magic Flute*.

1815 After the defeat of Napoleon, the seeds of a new Czech nationalism take root. A renewed interest in Czech culture leads to a revival of Czech as a written language.

1848 Nationalist fervor erupts in a student uprising against Vienna. After six days, the uprising is brutally suppressed.

1850–1914 The city industrializes. By 1914, 70 percent of the industrial output of the Austro-Hungarian Empire is produced in Bohemia, mostly in the greater Prague area. Prague becomes an international center of innovative art and architecture. Cubist and art nouveau buildings and design proliferate.

1918 The Austro-Hungarian Empire is dismantled. The Czechoslovak Republic is proclaimed under the Presidency of Thomas Garrigue Masaryk.

1918–1937 Dadaism, Surrealism, Constructivism, Poetism, Futurism, and Bauhaus ideas flower in the dynamic atmosphere of the new republic. Internal political tensions increase with the rise in power of the Soviet Union and Nazi Germany.

1938 The Munich Pact. The largely German Sudetenland is severed from Czechoslovakia. Slovakia becomes a quasi-independent state.

MARCH 15, 1939 Prague is occupied by the German armies. Reinhard Heydrich, later assassinated by the Czechs, is installed as *Reichsprotektor.* A reign of terror follows and the transportation of the Jewish communities of Prague, Bohemia, and Moravia to the concentration camps at Terezín begins.

MAY 5, 1945 The citizens of Prague rise up against the Germans. Four days later the Germans capitulate. Prague is liberated by the Soviet armies, while the United States Army remains in Pilsen. The Sudeten Germans are later expelled and their property confiscated. The Czech lands and Slovakia are reunited.

1946 The first postwar election. The Communists emerge as the strongest party with 36 percent of the popular vote.

FEBRUARY 1948 The Communist Party takes over the government. Prague recedes behind the Iron Curtain.

1951–1952 Show trials are held, in which leading members of the Czech Communist Party, many of whom are Jews, are purged and executed.

1956 The Twentieth Congress of the Communist Party of the Soviet Union is held in Moscow. Krushchev makes revelations about Stalin which initiate a movement toward reform. These reforms are slow to reach Czechoslovakia.

1968 The Prague Spring. The Czechoslovak Communist Party, under Alexander Dubček, institutes reforms. In August the Warsaw pact armies invade, putting a stop to the liberalization. A long period of repressive "normalization" begins.

1977 Václav Havel and other Czech and Slovak intellectuals form Charter 77, a human-rights group that becomes the core of unofficial, nonviolent opposition to the regime.

NOVEMBER 1989 Following the collapse of the Berlin Wall in East Germany and mass demonstrations in Wenceslas Square, the Communist government resigns. Václav Havel, recently released from a Prague prison, enters the Castle as president.

1990–1992 Democracy and a free market system are established. Under pressure from nationalist Slovaks, the country is divided by mutual agreement. Prague becomes the capital of the new Czech Republic.

1993–PRESENT Prague becomes a center of culture and enterprise once more. In the five years since the Velvet Revolution, much of the city is restored to its former beauty. Millions of tourists now visit Prague each year.

Glossary

Beneš, Edvard: Czechoslovak president from 1935 to 1938, when he abdicated under Nazi pressure, and again from 1943 (in exile) to 1948, when he abdicated under Communist pressure.

Bílá Hora: Literally "White Mountain," a hill on the outskirts of Prague (see above).

Bretschneider: Name of the secret police agent in *The Good Soldier Švejk* who arrests Švejk for *lese* majesty. Sometimes used, as it is in "The Little Bulldog," as a generic name for known police agents.

Břevnov: District of Prague west of Hradčany where the Battle of the White Mountain was fought in 1618. The "Star" Summer Palace (Hvězda) and the Game Park are located there.

Ferdinand Boulevard: Present Národní Třída.

Ferdinandstrasse: Same as above.

Franzenquai: Present Smetanovo nábřeží, or Smetana Embankment.

Gottwald, Klement: First Czechoslovak Communist president, in office from 1948 until his death in 1953.

Hácha, Emil: President of the post-Munich Czechoslovak Republic (1938–39) and then president of the Protectorate of Bohemia and Moravia (1939–45). He was arrested immediately after the cessation of hostilities in May 1945 and incarcerated in Pankrác Prison, where he died.

Heydrich, Reinhard: The *Reichsprotekor,* Hitler's number one man in Prague, and a main architect of the so-called "final solution" that produced the Holocaust. Heydrich was assassinated by Czech paratroopers in 1942.

Hrdlořezy: District on the outskirts of Prague; the name means "cut-throat."

Hus, Jan: *See* chronology.

Husák, Gustav: Slovak Communist politician and President of Czechoslovakia from 1975 to 1989.

Hussites: Supporters of Jan Hus in the religious campaigns fought after his death.

Karlsbrücke: German name for the Charles Bridge (Karlův Most).

Karlsgasse: Charles Street, or Karlova ulice.

Kreuzherrenplatz: Křižovnické náměsti, or square.

Laurenziberg: Petřín Hill.

Masaryk, Tomáš Garrigue: First president of the Czechoslovak Republic (*see* chronology), who served from 1918 to 1935.

Moldau: German name for the Vltava River.

Mühlenturm: German name for Staroměstské mlyny or the Old Town Mills.

Novotný, Antonín: President of Czechoslovakia from 1957 to 1968.

Postgasse: Present-day Karolina Světla Street in the Old Town.

Rudé právo: Official Communist Party daily in Czechoslovakia until 1990.

Samizdat: Literally "self-published." Under Communism, uncensored works of dissident writers continued to be published by the banned writers themselves in *samizdat* form. They were circulated underground, and often smuggled to the West for publication.

Schutzeninseln: Střelecký Ostrov, or Shooter's Island; an island in the Vltava near the National Theatre.

Smetana, Bedřich: Czech nationalist composer (1824–84).

Svoboda, Ludvík: President of Czechoslovakia from 1968 to 1975.

Zápotocký, Antonín: President of Czechoslovakia from 1953 to 1957.

Contributors

MICHAL AJVAZ (1949–) was born in Prague and graduated from Charles University. He has published two volumes of poetry and short prose sketches *(Murder in the Hotel International* and *The Return of an Old Lizard),* and a novel, *The Other City.* "The Past" is taken from *The Return of an Old Lizard,* published in 1991.

KAREL ČAPEK (1890–1938) was well known abroad during his lifetime. Amazingly prolific, he wrote novels, plays, stories, poems, travel books, newspaper columns, and essays. Many of his works have been translated and some have become classics of their genre, such as his play *R.U.R.: Rossum's Universal Robots.* "The Receipt" is one of Čapek's immensely popular "pocket tales," recently published by Catbird Press in a new translation by Norma Comrada.

IVAN DIVIŠ (1924–) is a poet and essayist who was born in Prague. During the 1950s and 1960s he worked partly as a laborer, partly in publishing; from 1960 to 1969, he worked for Mladá fronta publishing house. In 1968 he edited *Sešity,* a literary magazine. He emigrated to West Germany in 1969, where he worked for Radio Free Europe. He has published many volumes of lyric poetry both at home and abroad. "Invasion Day" is the title we have given to an excerpt from his memoirs, *The Theory of Reliability,* published in 1994 by Torst Publishers in Prague.

JAROSLAV HAŠEK (1883–1924) is best known for his comic novel *The Adventures of the Good Soldier Švejk,* one of the classic antiwar novels of the century. Hašek was a Bohemian in every sense of the word, and had a colorful career as an occasional journalist, a cabaret performer, political activist (he was a founding member of the Party of Moderate Progress within the Law), and bon vivant. Like his protagonist, Švejk, he ended up on the Russian front during World War I and contributed to the Russian Revolution as a Bolshevik commissar. "A Psychiatric Mystery" is one of the hundreds of stories he wrote throughout his career.

DANIELA HODROVÁ (1946–), a native of Prague, works at the Institute for Czech and World Literature. In addition to two works of criticism, she has written a trilogy of novels about Prague called *The Suffering City* and, in 1992, a monograph, *I See a Great City,* from which the prologue to this collection is excerpted.

BOHUMIL HRABAL (1914–) was born near Brno and is one of the most popular living Czech writers. He is best known in the West as the author of the story "Closely Watched Trains," on which the Academy Award-winning film of the same name was based. His stories, written in a pungent, literary version of vernacular Czech, recount the extraordinary lives of ordinary people. "The Hotel Paříž" sequence is taken from his novel, *I Served the King of England;* "The Magic Flute," his meditation on the student demonstrations in early 1989 is from a collection of shorter prose pieces called *November Hurricane,* published after the Velvet Revolution.

ALOIS JIRÁSEK (1851–1930) was a schoolteacher who became a major figure in modern Czech literature as the author of a large number of novels and stories that drew their themes and subject matter from Czech history and legend. His *Old Czech Legends,* first published in 1894, and from which "The Legend of the Old Town Clock" is taken, has recently been published in English by Unesco.

FRANZ KAFKA (1883–1924) was born and lived all his life in Prague. His friend, the literary critic Max Brod, wrote: ". . . a true son of Prague, Kafka had roots in the soil of Prague. His poetic soul was charmed by the mystical magic of the Old Prague and the mixture of her people. . . . [H]e had his roots in Czech and German culture, and also in the very ancient Jewish culture." Best known for "The Metamorphosis," and for his absurdist novels, *The Trial* and *The Castle*, Kafka also left behind many short stories, sketches, letters, and diaries. He wrote "Description of a Struggle" when he was twenty. It is practically the only piece he ever wrote with references to real places in Prague.

JIŘÍ KARÁSEK ZE LVOVIC (1871–1951) is the pen name of Antonín Karásek, poet, novelist, and literary critic, who for many years edited the influential journal *Moderní revue. Gothic Soul,* from which "Bells" is excerpted, appeared in 1900 and is a classic of the decadent symbolist phase of Czech fin-de-siècle literature. The nameless hero of this brief, plotless novella is the scion of a degenerate noble family who wanders about Prague looking for something meaningful to fill the emptiness of his days.

EGON ERWIN KISCH (1885–1948) was a Prague Jewish-German writer, journalist, and reporter for the Prague German-language newspaper, *Bohemia,* from 1906 to 1913. Although he was based for longer periods of time in Germany, France, the United States, and Mexico, he remains one of the quintessential Prague writers whose work captured the life and atmosphere of the city at a particular time in its history. The selection in this book is taken from one of the few books by Kisch ever translated into English, his autobiographical *Sensation Fair.*

IVAN KLÍMA (1931–) has written many novels, stories, and essays that are available in English. In 1968, during the Prague Spring, he was editor of the Writers' Union weekly. He was active in the literary *samizdat* scene throughout the 1970s and 1980s. His most recent publications in English include *My Golden Trades, Love and Garbage, Judge on Trial, Waiting for the Dark, Waiting for the Light,* and a collection of essays called *The Spirit of Prague,* the title piece of which is the epilogue to this book.

JIŘÍ KOVTUN (1927–) was born in the sub-Carpathian Ukraine but spent his childhood and youth in Prague. Shortly after the Communist takeover of Czechoslovakia in February 1948, he went into exile, eventually moving to the United States in 1973. Since 1977 he has worked in the Library of Congress in Washington, D.C., as a specialist in Czech literature. Kovtun is a poet, historian, novelist, and translator. His novel *Prague Eclogue,* which takes place during the Prague uprising at the very end of World War II, is about the fate of four young friends who become involved in the fighting in Prague. The first chapter, slightly abridged, appears in this collection.

FRANTIŠEK LANGER (1888–1965) was born in Prague, studied medicine, and for much of his life worked as an army doctor. He also wrote poetry, prose, and plays, and for a few years in the 1930s was dramaturge at the Municipal Theater in the Prague quarter of Vinohrady. He wrote several books of stories and puppet plays for children, although he was not primarily a children's author. The full title of his story in this collection is "The Prague Children and the Sword of St. Wenceslas." Written in 1940, it comes from his book *Prague Legends,* first published in 1956.

GUSTAV MEYRINK (1863–1932) was born in Vienna as Gustav Meyer. He was a banker with an interest in the occult and wrote satirical stories chronicling the decline of Austrian society. He moved to Prague, which became the setting for his most famous novel, *The Golem* (first published in 1915) and for other works, including his fantasy built around the life of English alchemist John Dee (*The Angel of the West Window*). Meyrink was popular in his time, then his work fell out of favor with both the Nazis and the Communists. There is a resurgence of interest in his work with the recent appearance in English of *The Green Face, The White Dominican, Walpurgisnacht,* and *The Opal and Other Stories,* and a new translation of *The Golem,* all published by Dedalus in England.

JAN NERUDA (1834–1891) was born in Malá Strana, the Prague quarter he lived in for most of his life and made the setting for his best-known prose work, *Malá Strana Tales.* Neruda was a practicing journalist and literary critic who also wrote poetry, plays, and stories that bring the city of his period alive. "What Shall We Do with It?" written for the Prague daily *Národní listy* in 1886, has remained to this day one of his most popular stories.

OTA PAVEL (1930–1973) was a sports journalist, reporter, and writer. He survived the war by working in the mines and, after the Communist takeover, worked in the sports department of Czechoslovak radio. He also wrote scripts for radio, television, and film. "A Race Through Prague" comes from one of his books of short stories, *How Father Walked Through Africa.*

KAREL PECKA (1928–) was born in Slovakia, studied in Bohemia and worked as a technician. In 1949 he was arrested by the Communists and spent eleven years in prison. On his release he worked as a stagehand in the National Theater, and since 1965 has devoted himself entirely to writing. During the 1970s and 1980s, he published his work mostly in *samizdat.* "The Little Bulldog" is taken from a collection of stories called *Malá*

Strana Humoresques, and along with two other stories, is currently being made into a full-length motion picture. It was first published by 68 Publishers in Toronto in 1985.

JOSEF ŠKVORECKÝ (1924–) was born in Náchod in northeastern Bohemia but spent most of his working life in Prague, until 1969, a year after the Soviet invasion, when he emigrated to North America and settled in Toronto, Canada. Škvorecký's major novels — which include *The Cowards, The Engineer of Human Souls, Miracle in Bohemia,* and the recently published *Republic of Whores* — are centered on the experiences of his protagonist, Danny Smiřický, and are immensely popular in the Czech Republic and widely read in many languages. During the 1970s, Škvorecký helped his wife, Zdena Salivarová, run 68 Publishers, an exile publishing house which put out hundreds of volumes of Czech literature banned inside the country. "Tenor Sax Solo from Washington" was originally written for the Prague daily *Lidové noviny* in early 1994 and expanded by the author especially for this anthology.

JINDŘIŠKA SMETANOVÁ (1923–) has worked as a magazine editor and story writer, publishing her essays, sketches, and stories in some of the major Czech literary magazines. In the 1970s she was unable to publish officially for political reasons and, like many banned writers, did menial labor to survive. "American Heating" comes from a collection of her work published in the late 1960s, called *A Bed of Roses.*

JÁCHYM TOPOL (1962–) was born in Prague and had a brief career as a singer and songwriter in an underground rock band in the late 1970s. In 1985 he co-founded *Jednou nohou* (*One Foot* [in Jail]), a *samizdat* literary review specializing in new Czech writing and literature in translation. The magazine later changed its name to *Revolver Review.* Topol now devotes himself mainly to his own writing. His first collection of poetry, *I*

Love You Madly, was published in *samizdat* in 1988 and received the Tom Stoppard Prize for unofficial literature. *Sestra (Sister),* his first novel, was published in 1994. "A Visit to the Train Station" is a shortened version of a story that originally appeared in *Revolver Review* in 1993.

Jiří Weil (1900–1959) was born near Prague and became a reporter, literary critic, translator, and novelist. He was a committed Communist when young, but was later expelled from the Party. To avoid being sent to a concentration camp during World War II, he went underground and later wrote about the experience in his novel, *Life with a Star. Mendelssohn Is on the Roof,* from which the excerpt in this book is taken, was published in 1960, a year after his death.

Translators

PAUL WILSON is a freelance journalist, translator, and editor, who lived in Prague for ten years. He has translated the work of leading Czech authors such as Václav Havel, Josef Škvorecký, Ivan Klíma, and Bohumil Hrabal into English. His most recent book-length translations include *The Republic of Whores* by Joseph Škvorecký, *The Spirit of Prague* and *Waiting for the Dark, Waiting for the Light*, by Ivan Klíma, and a book of speeches by President Havel, called *Toward a Civil Society*.

~

A. G. BRAIN is the pen-name of the Czecho-English translating team of Alice and Gerald Turner who made their name in the 1980s as translators of modern Czech prose. Among their published translations are the novel *Judge on Trial* by Ivan Klíma and *The Restoration of Order* by Milan Šimečka. They have recently translated Ludvík Vaculík's celebrated novel *Český Snář (The Dream Diary)*.

NORMA (BEAN) COMRADA has translated a wide range of works by Karel Čapek, most recently, *Tales from Two Pockets* (Catbird Press). She has published articles and given talks on Čapek's life and work. Currently she is editing a translation of Čapek's *Apocryphal Tales* and working on an anthology of Čapek's journalism, also for Catbird. She lives in Eugene, Oregon.

MICHAEL HENRY HEIM is Professor of Slavic Languages and Literature at the University of California, Los Angeles. He has translated a number of Czech authors including Bohumil

Hrabal *(The Death of Mr. Baltisberger, Too Loud a Solitude)*, Milan Kundera *(The Joke, The Book of Laughter and Forgetting, The Unbearable Lightness of Being, Jacques and His Master)*, and Jan Neruda *(Prague Tales)*. He also translates from Russian (Vassily Aksyonov, Anton Chekhov, Sasha Sokolov), Serbo-Croatian (Danilo Kis, Dubravka Ugresic), and Hungarian (Peter Esterhazy, Gyorgy Konrad).

PETER KUSSI has translated a variety of classical and contemporary Czech authors. He is the editor of several anthologies, including a Karel Čapek reader entitled *Toward the Radical Center*. He teaches at Columbia University in New York.

MIKE MITCHELL teaches German at Stirling University in Scotland, specializing in modern Austrian literature. He edited *The Dedalus Book of Austrian Fantasy* and translated the novels of Gustav Meyrink, H. Rosendorfer's *The Architect of Ruins,* and M. Mander's *The Cassowary.* In 1994 he was awarded the British Comparative Literature Association's translation prize.

MARIE WINN was born in Czechoslovakia and raised and educated in the United States. She has written twelve books and translated a variety of works from Czech, among them four plays by Václav Havel, an opera by Leoš Janáček, *Summer in Prague* by Zdena Salivarová, and *Mendelssohn Is on the Roof* by Jiří Weil. She is a regular contributor to the *Wall St. Journal.*

ALEX ZUCKER has worked as a translator/editor for Czechoslovak News Agency and as a copy editor for a Prague English-language weekly, *Prognosis.* He is currently working on a translation of Jáchym Topol's first novel, *Sestra (Sister).* He has also translated short stories by Jiří Stránský, president of the Czech PEN club. He lives in Prague and contributes translations to literary journals there.

Permissions